BOUND AND DETERMINED

Other books published by Learning Disabilities Worldwide

BOUND AND DETERMINED

To Help Children with Learning Disabilities Succeed

MARK COOPER, PH.D., L.P.C.

Learning Disabilities
Worldwide

In grateful memory of my mother, Cecilia C. Cooper, who taught me to reach beyond my grasp.
(1917–2001)

And in honor of the millions of struggling learners, who taught me a new meaning for heroism.

TABLE OF CONTENTS

FOREWORD

Bound and Determined is a book about hope for children with learning disabilities, their teachers and their parents. But it is more than that; it is a toolbox of practical strategies that can be used to transform frustrations into workable solutions and dreams into realities. Of the many authors who have written books on learning disabilities, none approaches the topic as Mark Cooper does. Dr. Cooper is a seasoned professional in the LD field. During his career of more than thirty years, Mark has been a teacher, counselor, and college professor . . . of equal importance, he is the parent of a child with learning disabilities *and* he has personally struggled with the challenging effects of a learning disability himself throughout his life. He is a highly respected professional in the LD field who knows first hand what having a learning disability can mean in one's life and in the life of a family.

There are books in the LD field that describe what it's like to have a learning disability and there are many books that detail various strategies to use in working with individuals who have LD. This book, however, is unique in that it very effectively combines both of these perspectives in a single, extremely insightful and resourceful volume. Most important, this book is exceedingly readable and is written with passion, vivid examples, and numerous useful suggestions that can be implemented by teachers, parents, or individuals with learning disabilities themselves.

The strategies offered throughout the book are very practical and can be easily employed without massive changes in school or home environments. Mark's advice is common sense and person-directed. In many cases, it involves a change in attitude and perspective more than widespread program adjustments. His recommendations include a sensitivity to the overwhelming loads that most teachers and parents carry. In short, this is a very "user-friendly" book.

In my thirty-five years in the field of learning disabilities, I have yet to encounter a book that is so effective in describing what it means to have a learning disability. The personal experiences of the author combined with his professional training as a counselor and LD expert allow him to write about things in ways that professionals alone or individuals with LD alone can neither fully comprehend nor adequately express.

Since the passage of the No Child Left Behind Act in 2001, schools have focused almost entirely on increasing the academic performance of all students, including those with disabilities. While achieving successful academic outcomes is certainly important, the overall growth, development, and well being of students involves much more than academic success. While teachers understand this, they now find themselves in an educational dynamic that does not encourage (and in some cases, does not even permit) emphasis on the non-academic dimensions of schooling. This book underscores the fact that understanding and addressing factors beyond academics is not only important . . . it is essential.

Learning is much more than a cognitive undertaking. It is also an emotional, affective, and visceral experience . . . especially for those who struggle to learn and remember. Mark understands this perfectly and has organized a book to address both the cognitive and emotional aspects of learning in a provocative, engaging, and visionary manner. Anyone who reads *Bound and Determined* will be transformed by its message and will view the condition of learning disabilities in a totally different light.

Just as Dr. Cooper powerfully argues that individuals with LD should be viewed by those who know and work with them as "gifts" and not "projects," so too, this book is a wonderful gift to the field of learning disabilities.

Donald D. Deshler, Ph. D.
University of Kansas
Center for Research on Learning
Lawrence, Kansas

Preface

I have a dream.

In my dream, children with learning challenges move mountains with motivation; taste defeat without quitting; replace thoughts of "I can't" with "I can"; utilize their resources; and take more risks.

I heard the sobs from a distance. It was not until I rounded the corner at the third-grade campus that I saw Bret sitting alone. His hands cupped around his chin, Bret was tightly clinging to his body. "Bret," I whispered. As he gazed upward, I could see his face wet with tears and his eyes soaked with hurt. As I placed my arms around him, he fell against my side as if to draw strength from my presence.

As Bret's sobs began to subside, he painfully spoke. "I'm not an I CAN kid. I can't make the A/B honor roll and be an Abbit." An Abbit was a special name in the school associated with children who earned A's and B's during a six-week period.

My thoughts shifted back to Bret's first-grade year when I was the resident counselor on his school campus, while on a sabbatical from the university where I taught. As resident counselor, I was there to accrue 2,000 internship hours toward completion of my requirements for a license in professional counseling. Bret listened to my exhortations during that year and the year to come that he and others were "I CAN" kids. Bret's severe problems with dyslexia did not stop him from agreeing and proudly proclaiming, "I am an I CAN kid!" His childlike confidence and enthusiasm bursting at the seams, Bret knew an I CAN kid could not do everything, but he knew that an I CAN kid could do something and that something could result in success.

I tried to jog Bret's memory and reassure him with talk of the old days when the school assemblies warmed his heart and the hearts of others with exclamations of "We are I CAN kids!" At the moment, those days seemed so far away. As I continued to struggle to find just the right comment to help rebuild that bridge between Bret and his previous I CAN thoughts, my racing thoughts came to a screeching halt upon hearing Bret whimper, "You just don't understand, Dr. Mark!"

A therapist is forewarned, "Never view a client as someone other than a client." Bret's whimper caught me off guard. Perhaps it was the resignation in his voice that echoed my own struggles as a young learner. Maybe it was the familiarity of the words that hit home. Whatever the trigger, Bret's expression of pain became my pain. His world suddenly became my world, and I could vividly recall what it felt like to look through the eyes of a child with a learning disability. I don't know what became bigger – the lump in my throat or the knot in my stomach. Both reflected the pain of that inner child crying, "I don't measure up!" The fact that I was a university professor, school consultant, licensed counselor, writer, and public speaker provided little comfort. At the moment, those accomplishments seemed to belong to someone else. I was just the kid with a learning disability.

Again, my thoughts shifted back to Bret. As I continued to nurture Bret with powerful antidotes to combat the resignation that too often impedes a child who experiences more pain than gain, I knew his difficult journey had just begun, along with about two and a half million other children diagnosed with learning challenges. I recalled a quote by Thomas Hodgkins, a physician, author, and activist, who wrote, "Failure is often God's own tool for carving some of the finest outlines in the character of his children." At this moment, Bret needed a tool. Failure alone will never enable Bret and children like him to persevere and succeed. Bret needed hope; the kind of hope described by Jerome Groopman, the author of The Anatomy of Hope. Groopman (2004) suggested that patient's who faced illness needed to acquire a true hope, a hope that complimented the genuine threat and danger of an illness with the genuine possibility that the illness could be overcome. Dr. Groopman found that patients with true hope needed a mental picture that reflected the assimilating of information about the illness and its potential treatment. According to Groopman, "But hope also involves what I would call affective forecasting – this is, the comforting, energizing, elevating feeling that you experience when you project in your mind a positive future" (193). To find true hope, Bret needed similar tools specially designed to combat his chronic thoughts of resignation and failure with sustained thoughts that his learning challenges could be successfully countered and his resignation minimized. In other words, Bret needed that comforting, energizing, elevating mental projection that reassured, "I have a positive future in sight." For Bret, the sighting of that positive future needed to be on that day.

Bound and Determined: *A Book Filled with Hope*

Bound and Determined is a book about hope for children with learning disabilities. Yet, it is more. Giving our children like Bret hope is an empty pipe dream if we do not teach them how to *achieve* that for which they hope. This book does that, too. It is a toolbox for parents, teachers, and individuals with learning disabilities to help make dreams come true. Dreams require from some of us more pain than gain. Is it fair? You bet it's not. Is it true? You know it is. Is it worth it? I wouldn't take less just as I wouldn't want Bret to take less.

Throughout *Bound and Determined*, there are references to children with learning disabilities, learning challenges, learning disorders, learning problems, struggling learners, and the like. Here the different terms are interchangeable. They represent children who process information in a way that complicates learning. The intent is to use the descriptors in the most general sense. There are millions of children who struggle with learning for various reasons. There are many learning experts who provide a variety of explanations for such learning challenges. In this book, the explanations for children's challenges are not nearly as important as the fact that the children face daily challenges with learning.

I have longed to make sense out of my daily challenges as a person who faced a learning disability that often crippled my mind, heart, and soul. Fortunately, in time, the trials, tribulations, and triumphs of my life became stepping-stones to success. They fed and nourished me and gave me hope. If the tools I have acquired can help smooth a trail for others to follow, my challenges will have been worthwhile.

Emergency Relief

It is not the number of children with learning disabilities that alarm me so much. I am more alarmed by the tens of thousands of children like Bret who express resignation, sadness, and shame at an early age and carry it for so long. Melia, a nine-year-old client came to my office for her third visit. A child with a learning challenge, her presenting problem was terminal failure. With tears rolling down her face, this young girl almost apologetically muttered, "My tears are bigger than the sun shines!" My heart cracked at such a dramatic expression by someone so young. Her despondent expression reflected her need for emergency relief with no time to waste.

But where is the emergency relief? I reflected. I watched how quickly emergency relief efforts were provided for drought victims in the Mississippi Delta, quake victims in California, hurricane victims in Florida, tornado victims in Kansas, flood victims in Texas, and the victims affected by the terrorism in New York and Washington. It is time for us to apply the Noah Principle: "No more prizes for predicting rain; just prizes for building arks." We can no longer afford to walk in waist-deep water in the middle of a storm holding umbrellas over our heads thinking, "This will protect and insulate us from the challenges." Our children with learning disabilities need and deserve more than that.

Emergency relief efforts for children with learning challenges are not as quick, nor as effective. This book contains emergency relief, in the form of timely messages, obstacles to anticipate and resist, and useful strategies designed for parents, teachers, civic and business leaders, and policy makers. This emergency relief cannot come soon enough since a higher percentage of students with learning disabilities drop out of high school than their peers without disabilities. In addition, many adults who grow up with learning challenges fare poorly in society, as they lack the daily living skills that would foster a more positive living environment. Many continue to be dependent on their families, facing either a high degree of unemployment or underemployment. Add to this their difficulties in social relationships, their lack of job satisfaction, their lack of high income and few opportunities for job and career advancement, and their prospects become even bleaker.

The relief efforts outlined in this book begin with the premise that all children can succeed and should be afforded every opportunity to do so. All children's dreams—including the dreams of children with challenges – must be recognized and nurtured. Fulfillment of one's dreams requires vials of encouragement and antidotes to obstacles to prevent the pervasive paralysis that often subdues, inhibits, or retards forward progress. I recall a coach screaming, "If you're going to fall, fall forward." All children fall at one point or another. Children with learning disabilities, however, fall more often than their non-disabled peers. It is our job to be there when they do and encourage them to fall forward.

Bound and Determined: *An Overview*

The first two chapters of this book are about my personal experiences of falling—falling forward. Through these chapters, I open my heart and bare my soul to parents, educators and others interested in understanding the minds of those who have learning disabilities. My trials, tribulations, and triumphs will be described from the very beginning—during early childhood through adulthood. There is never a time in my life when those earlier experiences as a struggling learner fail to affect my thinking.

Dr. Mark's Mental Messages for Success in the following chapter are based on the adage, "Thoughts breed feelings; feelings breed actions; actions breed character; and character breeds destiny." The destinies of children with learning challenges are bleak without thoughts (mental messages) of encouragement. Abraham, a five-year-old kindergartner, never stopped raising his hand when a question was posed to his class. "I know, I know, I know!" cried Abraham. Trust me; Abraham didn't know the answers to most questions. However, he never failed to believe in himself. Fourteen years later, Abraham was in college moving forward toward graduation. Abraham's thoughts were positive, and it showed in his character.

Dr. Mark's Messages urge readers to reframe their thinking about children with learning challenges. Each message is a "mental muscle" designed to strengthen children's ability to combat the negative thoughts, feelings, actions, and reactions that are part of their lives. At the same time, these "mental muscles" are designed to strengthen children's resolve to combat personal thoughts of resignation. The mental messages are very similar to Brooks and Goldstein's mindsets described in their very poignant book, The Power of Resilience. Brooks and Goldstein (2004), two of America's foremost clinical psychologists, suggested that mindsets are complex processes based on the interaction of one's unique temperament with one's life experiences. The authors are correct to reinforce the idea that mindset can change. The chapter on Dr. Mark's mental messages helps facilitate such change.

While I strike a note of optimism throughout the book, the obstacles that place children with learning challenges at risk of failure are not ignored. Chapter Four addresses many of the barriers that prevent children with learning challenges from reaching their full potential. These barriers include the propensity to categorize children based on their academic abilities, the application of a one-size-fits-all mentality where differential treatment is ignored, the pyramid mentality where children who perform the best receive the most praise and recognition, and more.

These barriers hinder learning because they adversely affect the mind, heart, and soul of the children. I know; I battled these barriers, and others, each and every day of my school years. I have also seen these barriers interfere with struggling learners as an educator and licensed professional counselor.

I cannot stand by and watch while these conditions persist in our schools, households, and communities. I cannot be "lukewarm" about teaching methods that rob children of enthusiasm, courage, motivation, and confidence. I cannot be apathetic about the internal bruises that suffocate the hopes of children and their desires to achieve success. Identification of the barriers is half the battle. Only when we truly understand these conditions as barriers can we formulate actions to combat their effects.

Action does not always guarantee that we achieve a particular goal. It does guarantee progress toward that goal or a new perspective to help a person reevaluate the goal. Dr. Mark's Strategies in Chapter Five are action-oriented. Here is where the rescue relief really takes form. The strategies presented here help parents and educators maximize their efforts, develop an action plan, and wisely use their time. Caring adults are provided with tools to help children with learning challenges climb the highest mountain and persevere through the lowest valley, find the will to never stop reaching and the hope to never stop dreaming. Dr. Mark's Strategies are designed to invite the passion required to wade ahead against strong currents. The application of such passion serves as a catalyst to help struggling learners combat low self-esteem, fear of failure, feelings of alienation, separation, and isolation, and a lack of motivation that are the everyday staples of these children.

A Meaningful Journey

Many years ago, during my twenties, I asked an elderly couple, "If you had it to do all over again, what would you do differently?" I watched them steal a glance at one another as if to wonder, "Is he ready for this?" They even appeared somewhat smug, as if they understood something that I, and perhaps many others, fail to understand. I waited patiently knowing they would answer in their own time. The wife took the lead. "There are three things," she began. I suspected this question had come up before. "First, I would stop more and smell the roses. Second, I would take more risks. And finally, I would do things that were more meaningful."

They were right. I was not ready for the answers. At that point in my life, I had too little time to stop and smell the roses. I viewed most risk-taking as just too risky. As far as the third suggestion, I thought she confused meaning with money. Presently, and with each passing year, I embrace the wife's reflections more fervently. As a person who intimately understands the thoughts and feelings of children with learning challenges, I have chosen to write this book with the hope it will make life more meaningful for these children and the parents and teachers who raise and teach them.

While I speak of an intimate understanding of children with learning disabilities, such understanding did not emerge without tremendous support among authors and nationally acclaimed speakers, such as Robert Brooks, Mel Levine, Larry Silver, Richard Lavoie, Don Deshler, Dale Jordan, Harold Levinson, and many more. The mental messages, the barriers, and the Dr. Mark's strategies echo the ideas shared by the aforementioned leading experts in learning disabilities. I have looked through the lenses of giants in the field. Their reflections should be evident.

I Too Have a Dream

Like Martin L. King, Jr., I too have a dream. I have a dream that all children with learning challenges learn to feel better about themselves, do their very best, and make perseverance their bosom buddy. In my dream, children with learning challenges learn to move mountains with motivation, embrace their abilities and inabilities, taste defeat without quitting, replace thoughts of "I can't" with "I can", utilize their resources, and take more risks. In my dream, the children's lives are filled with meaning and purpose. It is a wonderful honor for me to take a step toward the forefront and share such a dream.

I defied the very logic that says, "I can't achieve." The next several chapters are a compilation of my own personal experiences and training as well as the assimilation of ideas expressed in the speaking and writing of medical, clinical and teaching experts in the field of learning disabilities. It is my hope that the insight and information reflected in this volume will spark enough enthusiasm among parents and educators to instill in the minds, hearts, and souls of their children the same willingness to defy the logic that says, "They can't." In achieving that goal, I will understand that my struggles have been a blessing and I will find the ultimate meaning in my life—to help children with learning challenges not only to dream, but also to fulfill those dreams.

ACKNOWLEDGEMENTS

"I am as strong as we are." This mental message has guided me through a lifetime of experiences resulting in the book, *Bound and Determined*. I am grateful for the many children, families, and educators who contributed to the roots of my understanding about struggling learners.

For my development and the development of the book itself, I feel a deep sense of gratitude:

To my mom, Cecilia, you taught me to see beyond my present levels of performance and to see myself through your lens. Thank you for your divine patience and a willingness to meet me more than halfway.

To my wife, Linda, for 33 years you've been there for me. You have looked past the residue of my disabilities and affirmed me in every possible way. Thank you for your unconditional acceptance. Also, thank you for encouraging me to write in such a way that the reader feels the facts about the trials and triumphs of struggling learners.

To my daughter, Charlotte, you have demonstrated many thoughts and actions important to my teaching. You took a special interest in my efforts and never lost confidence in my work. Thank you for creating the title of the book. You knew me well.

To my son, Jim, you are a pivotal part of my learning and teaching. I find you more fearless than you will ever know. You taught me to see you first as a gift before I ever see you as a project. God continues to speak to me through the trials and triumphs of our relationship.

To my colleagues at the University of Central Arkansas in the Department of Early Childhood and Special Education, you have made my successes possible through your generosity. Your affirmation, affection, and acceptance have been greatly appreciated. You have allowed me to be who I am with little reservation.

To my first professional boss, Dr. Betty Caldwell, you introduced me to the idea that there was something great to champion – children. You taught me the importance of taking action. You also helped me set standards beyond my initial imagination. Thank you for such a vision.

To my L.P.C. supervisor and colleague, Dr. Michael Meyer, you provided me important feedback and encouragement designed to develop and sharpen my counseling skills.

To my friend, Janice Meyer, you taught me the role of intercessor for struggling learners, their families, and teachers. It was through you I learned most about the passion and resolve to champion children who struggle.

To my professional mentor, comforter, and spiritual advisor, Dr. Dale Jordan, you believed in me from the very beginning. Your correspondence with me has been invaluable. You epitomize the very special person in my life who embraced me unconditionally. I long to give to others what you have given to me. Thank you dearest friend.

To my personal editor, Veronica Zysk, you gave me the confidence to write when I did not feel like a writer. I appreciated your encouraging words, your tremendous demonstrations of excellence, your willingness to hold me accountable, and your critical analysis of my ideas. You truly made my work come alive.

To my friend and newest mentor, Dr. Don Deshler, you exemplify the highest level of integrity and passion to help others. I am thankful to be a recipient of such integrity and passion. You are a man of action, a man pure in spirit, and one who found a place for *Bound and Determined*. I will be forever grateful for such encouragement, commitment, and resolve.

To copy editor, Kirsten McBride, you offered your expertise and impressive skills of editing and writing. I appreciated so much the tremendous time invested in making *Bound and Determined* more reader friendly.

To my friend and the Executive Director of Learning Disabilities Worldwide, Inc., Teresa Citro, you are a dream maker and a dream shaper. I am thankful for your vision to make *Bound and Determined* possible. It will be through you that a new understanding about struggling learners emerges.

To copy editor, Moira Munns, you offered so much more than editorial and writing expertise. You offered your heart to me as a writer. You gave me so much encouragement in the midst of this project. You made me feel like a gift to potential readers.

CHAPTER ONE

SHHH, I HAVE A SECRET

Slowly a new way of thinking emerged. It became reassuring to know that tomorrow always represented another chance to succeed.

In The Beginning

I came into this world viewed as an agitator by some and as full of kindness by others—a classic example of the many contradictory traits that often reside simultaneously within a child with learning challenges. From an early age, I was a child who did not go unnoticed—not necessarily for positive reasons. As a result, my parents, friends, and even a neighbor adopted me as their "project" for years to come. Even before I was two years of age, people had strong reactions to my performance. It did not help that I called water "dorty." This unnerved one particular neighbor friend who kept insisting that I stop using such a word, when "wawa" was so simple.

This was my introduction to feeling dumb and my first realization that some people wanted to "fix me." While this neighbor remained agitated over my usage of the word "water," others found me quite charming. In the second grade, I would ask my classmates to stand when our teacher, Miss Baskin, entered the room. I didn't care that my seven-year-old peers thought my actions rather odd; wasn't this proper manners in the presence of a lady? In my mind it was. My social skills, although misplaced, were relatively sophisticated even then. By middle school, my nickname in our family had become the "peace-maker". I was the sibling most inclined to resolve arguments peacefully. I tried to quickly bring harmony to the surface following family conflict.

Very soon though, concern about academics overshadowed any interest the family had in my emerging abilities to bind people together. During a parent-teacher conference with Ms. McCall, my fourth-grade teacher, Dad blurted out, "I know he's a nice kid, tell me about his school work." Already I appeared to be lagging behind my classmates in reading and math. Feelings of being different—being less—were materializing as part of my world. I was becoming separate; feeling singled out for my lack of academic achievement. This was not something an aspiring fifth grader or a dad's son hoped would happen. "MY SON: THE PROJECT" was becoming stamped repeatedly across my forehead on its way to being forever ingrained in my soul.

I was not totally alone. There were three of us in class who looked and acted pretty much the same—lost. There were the two Danny's and me. We were the three miscues, the boys who failed to measure up in schoolwork. Grade after grade, I felt the excitement and joy of belonging to a class, this group of kids—

my comrades—steadily slipping from my grasp as the academic gap widened. I wasn't stupid. I knew something was wrong, and that something was named Mark. "Why me?" I often wondered.

A Walk Down Memory Lane

So began my quest to hide from my classmates. It was my protection, the magic potion that got me through the day. "Shhh, I have a secret," I started saying to myself. Secrets were not good to keep as a young child; telling the truth was an important lesson. And, for the most part, I was a very obedient child. Obedience was something I could be good at. What a heavy weight this secret would become in my life; what a burden it was to carry.

A school day resembled a walk in the jungle, with all my efforts concentrated on just surviving the day. "Walk softly and the animals may not hear me, hide and they might not see me," I'd think. School was filled with hourly threats to my existence, except the wildlife were adults and classmates. Rather than being my refuge, the classroom became a threat to my safety. At every turn danger lurked. There were predators ready to seize upon my weaknesses.

An example of that danger involved the spelling bees that took place far too often. One week can seem like eternity or just a stone's throw away. In this case, it was the latter.

"Here we go again," I thought, while listening to the teacher introduce the next fifteen spelling words in preparation for our weekly test.

"Mark, if you study real hard every day, you will do well on Friday's spelling test." Why does she have to make it sound so easy? Her benign encouragement provided little relief for my growing frustration. My feelings didn't improve when a classmate yelled, "Oh, these are easy words! Anybody can spell these."

"Anybody, but me." His words seared into my mind, burning holes in an already thin shell. I slumped down further in my seat, as my heart sank through my chest. Spelling was not my best subject. Actually, it was one of my worst. I hated the Thursday morning spelling bees even more. Thursday gave me another chance to fail in front of the entire class and endure their ridicule.

Another classmate sang boldly and confidently, "I can't wait for the Thursday spelling bee. My team is gonna' win." I sat there wishing I had even the smallest bit of her confidence. Why couldn't that be me? And then the worst of my worst fears echoed yet again, as a third classmate whispered loudly in response, "Unless we have you-know-who on our team." Fortunately, there was only a one-in-three chance that comment was directed toward me. There were two other students who spelled worse than I did. Sad to say, I occasionally retorted, "yeah," hoping to deflect anyone's perception that person might be me.

Monday, Tuesday, and Wednesday evenings were a double-edged sword: time to prepare and a breeding ground for anxiety. Three days was not much time; at least, it was not much time for me. But the fear of looking dumb in front of my classmates had become a catalyst for tremendous self-motivation. I was bound and determined to learn the words. Luckily for me, my mom was bound and determined to teach me.

"Just do your best," Mom insisted, night after night. "What does my best look like?" I wondered silently. It wasn't part of my daily repertoire. My best never appeared to resemble the best among others.

I didn't resist Mom's help. I wasn't stupid; I knew Mom was necessary, and she was always available. She knew her "project" and with each passing instance we shared she was refining her technique for turning it into a success. Each time I'd utter, "I don't know" or "I can't," Mom was there with patience and persistence. I hated making mistakes. I had made so many, so often, and felt their bitter sting so incessantly that I could no longer separate the mistake from my own sense of worth. As a result, I seldom tried to spell words unless I knew I could do it right. Risk-taking was not part of my vocabulary at that time in life.

"Go ahead and try. Just do your best," Mom coaxed. There it was again, my "best"—hanging like a two-ton weight around my neck. Damned if I do and damned if I don't. So, I'd try and invariably we'd repeat the same pattern: I'd miss the word, Mom would spell it correctly, and I'd spell it correctly—for the time being. Double humiliation, destined to repeat itself. Over and over Mom would tell me to "do my best", and over and over I'd have to risk failure to make even the slightest progress. At the end of many evenings, I'd fall asleep playing back words in my mind. In my weaker moments, I told myself, "I'm not good at this." However, I had somehow learned that this type of thinking did nothing but pull me down further and faster into the failure abyss. These moments of resignation didn't thwart my persistence to be prepared. I knew, from an early age, that working hard was preferable to some of the worse things I had experienced—including doing poorly in front of your classmates.

Wednesday evenings were the hardest. My facial tics and body contortions really came alive then. Whenever possible, I'd reserve their expressions for outside of class. It was bad enough feeling stupid during the spelling bee, I didn't want to look stupid too. So much of my time was spent trying to hide parts of myself from others. Thursday morning was filled with anticipation. My anxious feelings and restlessness became even stronger. It was the day of reckoning. "O.K. boys and girls, let's see how much you have studied," our teacher challenged. Surely, the teacher knew that some children's performances did not always reflect the amount of study. "Didn't she?" Many of the children celebrated the announcement; I didn't. This was my time to blend into the woodwork, to don my invisibility shield.

Every spelling bee had teams. The teacher usually selected the top-two spellers to choose their teammates. As if misspelling a word in front of my peers wasn't bad enough, the selection process was even worse. "Pick me, pick me!" several classmates exclaimed. I never competed as a high lottery selection, so I anticipated each choice with a sinking feeling in my stomach. The confident, self-assured students always seemed so excited. They'd all clap their hands, jump up and down, and squeal with delight as their names were called early on. The lower-round picks, like me, were not greeted with such enthusiasm. In fact, the disappointed looks on the faces of the already-selected teammates were rarely hidden. Although the teacher's occasional stare and glare stopped classmates from expressing too much dissatisfaction at us "benchwarmers."

Even after my name was called, the walk from my desk to the huddled team felt like descending into a black hole. The classmates were already preparing their strategy. "You could have waited for me," I thought. However, I didn't want them looking at me anyway. Being invisible amidst their sea of words was just fine with me. Sometimes I'd sneak a look at the other comrades who shared my spelling difficulties. Judging by the looks of fear and intimidation on their faces, I suspected their moms did not help them like my mom did me.

The spectacle would begin, as our teacher lined up students in no particular order. It felt like a firing squad. Thank God she did not line students up by expectation. She'd challenge, "Felicia, spell hide."

"Oh, that's so easy," cried several classmates. I hated them for saying that. And I hated the grunting sounds they'd make during even the slightest hesitation by the speller. I fretted over the word selection as the teacher gave out the second word. "What word will I get?" I wondered.

Sometimes the teacher asked some of us to spell easy words. Maybe she thought it was merciful. I recall my side screaming with delight as if they had just witnessed a miracle. "Way to go, Mark!" they echoed, as I completed a word successfully. The bullet missed. This time!

"That's not fair. That's an easy one. Why can't we get easy ones like that?" The opposing team's displeasure was obvious. They were banking on me for points. Even when I spelled a word correctly, it didn't feel much like an accomplishment.

The harder words—at least, words hard by my standards—were my worst nightmare. Even a nanosecond of hesitation was met with a chorus of grunts and groans or proclamations of "I know! I know!" I just wanted to hide; I didn't want everyone to look at me. My stupidity was out there on center stage, naked for everyone to see. "I don't know" became my safety net. The classmates tended to be more forgiving when I gave in than they were of my efforts to "do my best" when I failed. I also learned the hard way that certain classmates found more humor in misspelled words, and readily expressed it.

Yet, I remember celebrating our victories alongside my teammates, regardless of my contribution or lack thereof. In fact, I would join in, chiding the opposition for losing. Why not? That's what my classmates did when they won; was I that different? But our losses were not that easy to forget. The good spellers always had their reasons for losing. While the teacher never heard them, I did. "We would have won if it were not for you-know-who."

The next day we'd have our weekly written spelling test, and I'd feel thankful that at least no one would see my performance but me. For six more glorious days—until the next spelling bee—I could keep my secret to myself. I could hide behind individual assignments and become part of the nebulous sea of classmates. Just long enough to regain some inner composure and prepare for next week's public spectacle where my secret would once again be exposed.

But the spelling bees were not the only dangers lurking around corners. The reading groups, board work, assignment comparisons, and small group assignments were all like snakes, always present and ready to strike. I longed to scream, "Snake!" and have someone come to my rescue. But who would notice? Only the two Danny's would even understand the anxiety that filled every hour of every day. There were no rescue parties out there to protect me. Never did someone at school come forward to offer me aid.

Traditionally, the school environment is rich with experiences that draw comparisons among students. Report cards are one example. Every six weeks I was held up for inspection. Did I compare favorably with other kids? Was I a success or a failure? As the hours passed on report card day, I became increasingly anxious. The end-of-the-school-day bell would ring, signaling it was time for the after-school show-and-tell to begin.

I never had bragging rights on report card day. Who in their right mind would brag about average grades, even though such grades required a huge effort on my part and an even bigger effort on Mom's part? Even when my grades were acceptable, deep down inside I still heard the now-familiar voice opposing the success. "Boy, the teacher sure gave you a bone with the B. You know you're not that smart—not really. You're just trying to hide how dumb you are. Do you really think you can get away with it? Yeah, right."

Spelling bees were weekly torture, but performing at the chalkboard was perhaps the most traumatic experience during school years. There are few activities more stressful or humiliating for a child with academic difficulties than standing before his or her peers and making major, stupid mistakes. Usually there were four of us in front of the class at a time, waiting to work on a problem on the board. I was so extremely self-conscious. The demons in my mind were even worse than the ones I could see. I was usually rewarded for my inability to perform with the occasional snicker from a classmate which did not help while I was earnestly trying to solve the problem.

How could I be expected to handle a board problem when the real problem was fifteen classmates staring? As if that was not bad enough, the teacher made the situation even worse by asking the class, "Can anyone help Mark?" I felt like I was wearing a sign that flashed, "Stupid, stupid, stupid." Of course, most of the students in the class would vigorously wave their hands, making grunting sounds or yelling out, "I know! I know!" The teacher was quick to reward those classmates with a cheerful look, an illuminating smile, and wonderful words of encouragement. "You are right, Edith. Say it again for Mark." Not only would I be standing there humiliated because of my mistake, the teacher would keep me at the board, waiting until I demonstrated understanding. Even after I was given the correct answer, understanding was often not quick to come.

Shhh, I Have A Secret

The message of Harold Levinson (1984), author of *Smart But Feeling Dumb* and the more recent *Total Concentration* (1990), was lost on me. While I stood at the chalkboard or participated in spelling bees or reading groups, there was nothing running through my mind that said, "Gosh, Mark, you are smart but feeling dumb." The thought was more like, "I'm feeling dumb and acting dumb." There was nothing smart about my feelings or actions in front of my classmates. Of course, Levinson was accurately suggesting how many students with learning disabilities are, in fact, smart, but feeling dumb. In my case, I just felt dumb.

These were the moments when I wanted to hide, to don some shield that would make me invisible to the world. These moments reinforced my need to keep my struggles with reading, writing and spelling a secret. The anguish connected with classroom work flared up many times each day, like the red hot fire of an active volcano spewing forth a molten lava that burned to a crisp my already fragile ego and left a trail of negative thoughts. At that early age, I failed to understand why I felt the way that I did. Pretty quickly I learned more and more ways to hide my truth, to keep my shortcoming a secret from as many people as possible.

Rejoicing the Good Times

Thank God I excelled at sports. I was usually picked first on the basketball court or football field. I guess God felt I needed to have something going for me! I was blessed with as much physical ability as anyone during my elementary school years, despite being the shortest child in school. Although I was only four feet nine inches tall going into high school, it didn't interfere with any athletic ability. Sports contributed immensely to my social life. I was often elected class officer and served on the student council. I seemed to have some natural leadership qualities, but they were not given much importance compared to reading, writing, and arithmetic.

I acquired two very close friends early on and together we created many fond memories. The close bonds I had with Rodney and Chris helped me accept myself despite my shortcomings. Rodney and I were at opposite ends of a spectrum. He made excellent grades, but did not fare well in sports. I made average grades, but was great at sports. We were the best of friends. Chris was also a best friend, who provided great protection for my suffering ego. The time our coach asked me to call out my shoe size (let's just say it was another way I didn't measure up) in front of all the jocks, Chris took charge of crowd control when the laughter broke out by yelling, "Be quiet and mind your own business." Unconditional love and acceptance surged among the three of us. As I look back, I realize how important those friendships were for my self-esteem, especially as a struggling learner.

Family life also provided some respite from the daily strain of the school environment. I loved my family and never remember feeling like an outcast with them. At times my sisters rescued me at home, since my language development was delayed. As the story goes, before I had a chance to open my mouth to say anything, they jumped in and said it for me. They also rescued me from answering the phone. I am not sure if the rescue was designed to support me or to prevent the possibility of me making a verbal mistake with one of their friends. For the most part, I remember support among my siblings and enjoyed their company. This was especially true with my brother, Randy, because of the hours and hours of playtime we spent together. There never seemed to be anything but acceptance between us until adolescence. Once he beat me in tennis, I stopped playing. Little brothers are not supposed to dominate big brothers in sports.

Parental Support: A Mixed Bag of Emotions

The interactions with Mom and Dad were a grab bag of emotions. It became obvious very early in life that school performance was a valued commodity in the Cooper household. Although my father's pediatric practice kept him away from home much of the time, he maintained a high level of interest in all my academic endeavors. I could sense, even in elementary school, that my lagging grades and academic difficulties were upsetting to him. He often tried to assist me with homework, but to no avail. His patience crumbled when his explanations were not immediately understood and learned. Our efforts usually ended in mutual frustration, tension, and anger. It didn't take long for Dad's voice to change from supportive to argumentative, to intolerant.

Mom, however, was the rock in my life. Her quiet, timid nature belied her inner strength and determination. When the school discovered I had a reading problem, Mom took a reading course to be able to help me better. When the math problems surfaced, she took a special education course. She did not know at the outset that her efforts to assist me with my significant academic difficulties would lead her to finish a master's degree in reading with a specialization in special education. She changed careers from a registered nurse to an educator of children with learning disabilities.

We spent endless hours together, preparing each evening for the next day. While my friends were outside playing, I was frequently working with Mom, or one of the many tutors my parents hired to guide me through my academic years. I remember a time when a friend said, "You sure must make great grades with all the time you spend studying." While my grades may have been decent, I didn't feel they were very redeeming, considering the investment of time and the trade-offs I had to make. I began to realize that the grades were not mine— they were Mom's and a little bit of mine. Every piece of homework was checked and rechecked for errors before it was finished. Every essay or paper was scrutinized for spelling errors and comprehension. My sisters joked that Mom practically wrote all my papers for me. It was partly true, and I knew it.

I came to view Mom and the tutors as my support system, created and designed to specialize in my future and me. No matter how much I didn't want to study, didn't want to deal with making mistake after mistake after mistake, I knew they were important. My aunt Carol once remarked, "I'd come over to visit and, invariably, find you and your mom working at the dining room table for hours at a time."

Despite ambivalent feelings about working with Mom, I knew I couldn't survive without her. I became determined, tenacious, and tireless about schoolwork. Why not? How else could I keep from being discovered? She helped me keep my secret of feeling dumb, but acting smart. With her help, I could achieve decent grades and appear to my classmates at least moderately smart. How I appeared to myself was another matter. Neither mom nor the tutors had a study program that attacked my feelings of stupidity and anxiety.

Feeling Dumb But Acting Smart: A Learned Behavior

Little by little, I became increasingly skillful at feeling dumb but acting smart. I made small, but meaningful, advances in my schoolwork. And slowly a new way of thinking emerged. For whatever reason, perseverance became my bosom buddy and tenacity my closest ally. My persistence became akin to a security blanket, and it became reassuring to know that tomorrow always represented another chance to succeed rather than another day to fail. The possibility of thinking—and later, believing—that success was within my grasp, despite inner voices to the contrary, became a new reality for me. It was then that I began to better appreciate Levinson's book title, *Smart but Feeling Dumb*.

I Am The Emerging Project

It was during these later elementary school years that Mom and Dad started taking me to "specialists" for evaluations. Why was it that their child, who was very good in some areas, who was socially competent and truly tenacious, had such difficulties in certain academic areas? They wanted the mystery solved; they wanted answers that could explain away my "problems", my "challenges", my "deficiencies". I felt as if I was continually under the microscope of examination, with mixed reviews from psychologists and doctors in Arkansas, Texas, Louisiana, Mississippi, and Pennsylvania.

After visits to approximately six different professionals in various states, I was finally diagnosed with dyslexia at age fourteen. The upside to these visits was that Mom and Dad were encouraged by the diagnosticians to recognize my strengths. I sensed some relief in Dad that my condition had a name. I believe he began seeing me as a person with abilities rather than a child who had cornered the market on disabilities. Mom, with her unconditional acceptance of me already in place, was propelled to further action. And for myself, I just kept working toward my goals: secrecy, survival, and even a little success.

While my parents and some of my teachers began to feel confident in my potential, I, on the other hand, was becoming acutely aware of their sense of me as a planned undertaking. Never before had I felt so much like their project. The diagnostic examinations seemed endless and further reinforced my fear that "fixing me" was an agenda they all shared. "When will I no longer be under the microscope?" I wondered. I was continually under scrutiny, or better said, my performance was. They hardly ever noticed the real me; it was always what I was doing—or not doing—that captured their attention. I was a patient who needed healing, a problem who needed a solution, and a person who needed a better identity. This was a time in my life that I wanted to be enjoyed, appreciated and celebrated. Unfortunately, no diagnostic examination called for such a prescription. I arrived at those examinations being viewed as a project and always left wearing those same clothes.

There were peaks and valleys in my subsequent achievements. Junior and senior high school were characterized by more trips down the mountain than up. My need for instructional help didn't dissipate. There were many, many moments when I experienced strong feelings of resignation, some lasting longer than others. During the school year, we kept up our rigorous schedule of homework with Mom's help and outside tutors. During the summer months, I attended camps that offered academic programs in the morning and either sports or free time in the afternoon. As a team we were resolved that I should be given every opportunity to learn and succeed; as an individual, I was still battling my demons at every turn. However, now I was being given armor and weapons to fight these inner demons of doubt and negative thoughts. It helped.

The Diagnosis: A Sigh of Relief

The ultimate summer experience occurred at the Scottish Rites Hospital in Dallas, Texas, when a team supervised by Dr. Lucious Waites reaffirmed the diagnosis of dyslexia. Because of Dad's relationship with both Dr. Waites and the hospital, the weight of their diagnostic seal resulted in renewed determination to pursue improvement in my classroom performance. Mom and I spent six weeks in Dallas while I attended a specialized reading program for adolescents with dyslexia. Mom spent the time learning how to specialize in me.

This experience became a pivotal period in my life. For the first time, my school-related problems were explained. My shortcomings did not look so bad when paired with the explanation that I was a child with a learning disability. It sure was better than being dumb; I had just been an academic "ugly duckling." I now had a reason to accept myself, to embrace all that was I, including my shortcomings. By the end of that summer, Mom and Dad realized I had the potential to compete academically. So did I; things started to shift.

My academic self-doubt did not dissipate upon entering college. By this time it wasn't only my parents and teachers who had adopted me as their project; the idea had been firmly, albeit unconsciously, ingrained in my own thinking, too. A biology professor who reviewed my ACT scores predicted that I would not do well in college. Once again, how I did, or did not, measure up on a standardized examination in comparison to other students was being used to predict my individual capabilities. Too often, this near-sighted and myopic vision ruins many youngsters. Yet, despite the professor's cynical forecast, I completed my bachelor and master of science degrees at a small university over a five-year period. After several years of teaching with Dr. Betty Caldwell, a renowned pioneer in early childhood education, I began thinking about a doctoral degree. But the mere thought of becoming part of a class with other Ph.D. students created a great deal of anxiety. "Was I capable? Could I do this? Was I smart enough?" These and other negative thoughts played over and over in my mind. I was driven to prove myself, to prove my ability to overcome, to succeed, if not to others, at least to myself. Old habits die hard; in my case, this one would live with me forever. Unfortunately, at that time it felt more like a curse than a blessing.

A larger, more competitive university with other doctoral candidates was a bit too much for me to grasp. It was very hard to ignore my highly vocal demon, self-doubt. As I discussed the prospect of pursuing the degree with Dad, I could tell he was equally unsure about the feasibility of such a decision. He wanted what I wanted; however, he was still my dad trying to insulate me from the hurt that accompanies rejection and failure.

Head to Head Combat with My Hopes, Dreams, and Reality

I decided to test the waters by taking two graduate courses in the psychology department at a major university in North Carolina during the 1970's. What a frightening experience it turned out to be. I had grown accustomed to making good grades at the smaller university in Arkansas and expected the same at the larger more competitive university out-of-state. I remember studying six to eight hours a day during the week and ten hours a day on weekends, and still performing low C work on the first exam.

I was bitterly disappointed. My inner demons were relishing their new-found opportunities to emerge again, and their voices were louder than ever before. When I did no better on the second test, the professor suggested that I see him about my grades. I lamented to him how upset I was over my average. His only retort was that it was extremely difficult to obtain As and Bs in the psychology department at this particular university. As I closed his office door behind me, I remember thinking that here was the "real world", where my grades really counted. Of course, I did not measure up. Why was I surprised? However, the early determination and tenacity that had developed as a child had turned itself into a tenacious dedication to prove my ability to succeed. I ended up with B's in Experimental Psychology and Developmental Psychology and left the courses armed with enough self-assurance to pursue a doctorate.

I immediately applied to a major university in Texas in hopes of working with an outstanding early childhood educator, Dr. Joe Frost. To help me prepare for my Graduate Record Exam, I began seeing one tutor to help build my vocabulary and another to help me with math. These were very humbling experiences, as my math tutor was not only smarter, but also younger, a high school student teaching a prospective Ph.D. candidate. It was not quite as bad, however, as working with a pre-medical student every night, going over 1,000 vocabulary words. I hated this exercise with a passion; it made me feel so inferior.

Despite my hard work, my Graduate Record Exam scores were less than adequate. Nevertheless, I was optimistic about getting accepted at the university because of my good professional reputation. During the first several years of teaching, I became very well respected as an excellent teacher. I also became actively involved in a project designed to help promote social and emotional learning among children. This project resulted in numerous speaking engagements and the publication of a book entitled *AWARE: Activities for Social and Emotional Development.*

Since my optimism for acceptance was high, I spent few moments anticipating anything other than a favorable response from the university. Their rejection was painful; even more so because it came in the form of a telephone call, rather than a polite, impersonal letter. I can still taste the pain today when I think of that call. REJECTED! It was like indelible ink stamped on my soul forever. Not long after, I received some great advice from Dr. Frost. He said, "Mark, never look back. Let this be our loss, not yours. You have the ability; keep applying."

Despite the low G.R.E. scores, I was finally accepted into a Ph.D. program at a large university in Georgia. Dr. Walt Hodges, another prominent leader in early childhood education, was part of the interviewing committee. I wanted to work with Dr. Hodges, and knew my inadmissible G.R.E. scores would surface during the interview. They did. I looked each member of the committee squarely in the eyes and said, "These scores reflect my weaknesses, no more and no less. They do not represent my strengths. Give me a chance and let me demonstrate my capabilities."

By this time I had grown a bit weary of other people's adherence to test scores. I had started out an agitator, and once again, this trait came to my rescue. The good news was that I was accepted. The unforeseen bad news was the effect it had on me. I felt as if I carried the burden of every student in the world who was accepted with unimpressive G.R.E. scores. The committee had taken a chance on me; I was afraid to do anything short of succeeding, so others coming after me with low test scores might be accepted, too. It was a monumental weight to carry on my shoulders. It must have been four years into my program of study before I expressed to Dr. Hodges my feeling of immense responsibility. He helped me gain perspective and release some of this burden.

The Ultimate Challenge

The Ph.D. program was harder than anything I had experienced. While I had come to trust my abilities in the work world, I still didn't see myself as a good student. My imagination would run rampant, making the workload even more challenging than it was. Fortunately, I found myself in good company, since many excellent students shared my feelings of incompetence. This camaraderie helped me to keep my insecurities at bay and I finished my studies with good grades.

It was when the comprehensives came along that my insecurities intensified beyond anything I had known previously. I failed the first of three comprehensive examinations. Following the defeat, I told Dr. Hodges something that few people beyond my family at the time knew: that I had a learning disability. This fact typically stayed in the closet. Perhaps I was looking for a reason to excuse myself from the rigorous demands and expectations of my professors. It didn't work. Dr. Hodges appeared unsympathetic and insensitive. He would not lower his expectations any more than he would allow me to lower mine.

Two factors contributed to the successful completion of the second attempt. First, my wife, Linda, and two very close friends, David, and Jim, rallied to my cause and offered the emotional support that I needed. Second, a faculty member on my doctoral committee gave me some invaluable advice. Dr. Weld asked, "Mark, what were you thinking when trying to answer your four questions regarding the statistics, measurement, and research comprehensive?" I explained to Dr. Weld that I imagined the gap between my answer and the expectations of the committee responsible for grading the answers. At that time, Dr. Weld explained that my perception of the gap was very likely far smaller than meets the eye. In other words, he encouraged me to see a smaller gap by giving me more credit and giving them a bit less credit. He also encouraged that I represent my very best and feel confident that my very best will measure up. Of course, I had listened to that exhortation for years from Mom. Dr. Weld was right. I attacked the next comprehensive with new insight. I represented my very best and imagined my best answers to four more questions were not appreciatively different from those who graded the answers.

While I had attained the coveted doctoral degree, Dr. Hodges had given me a much more valuable lesson. He knew something that I failed to grasp at the time. He knew I could pass the comprehensive, even when I didn't. He was as determined not to give up on me, as he was to make sure that I did not give up on myself. More people are needed who have both a willingness to set high expectations for students with learning challenges, and the confidence in the person's ability to meet those expectations.

I pledged an allegiance to stop this pursuit of academic performance. I was tired of trying to chase the pot of gold at the end of the rainbow called self-acceptance and self-affirmation, especially since the self-acceptance and self-affirmation were yoked to academic excellence. The pledge lasted several years. However, it did not last a lifetime.

Searching for Success in All the Wrong Places

In the early 1990s I began pursuing licensure in professional counseling. A most poignant time followed: thirty-six graduate hours, a 400-hour practicum, the 2,000 internship hours, and finally, the licensing examination. As I shared the news of passing the licensure exam with my sister, Kristin, she shone the light of truth on my situation when she exclaimed, "Mark, are you through?" The comment caught me off-guard and my enthusiasm waned. I questioned, "What do you mean am I through?" Kristin chided, "Are you through trying to prove yourself because we are tired of worrying about you?"

At that point, I understood exactly what she meant, and we both chuckled. Her comment awakened me to the realization that while I was worrying about my performance, she was worrying about me. To Kristin, I was a person. Me? I still couldn't let go of myself as a project, one that under no circumstances could fail.

This walk down memory lane highlights the experiences that affected my thoughts and actions. While the experiences planted seeds of self-doubt and feelings of resignation, they also became a catalyst for the emergence of determination, tenacity, and a willingness never to give up.

CHAPTER TWO

THE TRUTH SHALL SET YOU FREE

Go forth and prepare yourself with a mighty team, led by your mighty thoughts designed to filter the negative and feed the positive.

The gold medallion of human worth too often goes to one of three competitors—brains, money, or beauty. While unfortunate, it is true. People tend to bemoan what they don't have more than celebrate what they do have. Those who have less money are frequently those who complain about wanting more. Those who consider themselves less attractive find creative ways to improve their looks. Those who see themselves as less intelligent frequently work to improve their superiority or compensate to hide their inferiority.

Chapter One's walk with me down memory lane gave away my nemesis— brains over brawn and money. This is not to say I possessed financial security or great looks. However, it was the struggles in school that challenged my thinking the most. Six hours per day, five days a week for many, many grades children are compared one to another and children make comparisons among one another. This is especially difficult to struggling learners. Brains quickly become the gold medallion for those children, often because it represents a commodity that is highly rewarded in school.

For me, the movement from hiding to disclosure has come slowly but surely. I have never been satisfied to allow feelings to regulate my actions. That is, not since my childhood and adolescent years, when I began to reframe my thinking to hold my demons at bay. Throughout college, graduate school, and into my professional life, the various strategies I'd put together began helping me through the ever-present whispers of doubt and the insecurities that filled my daily thoughts.

The completion of my Ph.D. did little to hush the whispers of doubt. For my first professional employment I selected a regional university in Beaumont, Texas. There seemed to be a good fit between my inner demons and the expectations of the university. There was no publish-or-perish climate at this institution. The inner drive to achieve was enough motivation. Given my well-practiced need to prove myself, I began publishing. I demonstrated teaching excellence, advised a dormant student education organization on campus to national prominence within three years, and developed highly regarded programs for children during the summer months.

Although others may have perceived that I achieved such successes with apparent ease, secrecy was still a pervasive element of my life. I kept secrets as protection. Acting smart, yet feeling dumb was the persona that had become as familiar to me as my own skin. It made me less vulnerable, but the tension it created in its wake was deeply felt. I was still in the jungle, always on the lookout for wild animals and hidden traps. It had just become a different jungle.

One such jungle I remember was on the campus of a small private college in Arkansas. I prepared to attend a three-week institute on children and adolescents with learning disabilities. It was a select group—only twelve professionals. For me, it was a chance to be a student for two weeks and a presenter for one. The following experience reflected the unfinished business that perverted my thinking, feelings, and actions as well as inhibited a freedom to be me.

Over an early morning breakfast, I exchanged informal introductions and enjoyed light conversation with other participants. Amidst the usual posturing, I surveyed the institute candidates; the strength of their expertise and credentials was impressive indeed. My body posture stiffened. There it was again; that old familiar voice in my head saying, "What can I teach these people whose expertise extends beyond my own?" Thank God, this was not the week for my presentation.

I left breakfast earlier than the other participants, cutting off the opportunity for my inner voice to continue its anxiety-provoking comparisons between "them" and me. The walk from the cafeteria to the conference room took less than ten minutes. It was a glorious day, with a clear, blue sky and a cool breeze —a perfect chance to settle down and clear my mind. But as hard as I tried to enjoy the tranquillity and peace of my surroundings, the mental static would not rest. My inner voice of doubt charged on. "Mark, what do you know about students with learning disabilities that qualifies you to participate in such an institute? What can you possibly teach these people, whose abilities and qualifications exceed your own? What were you thinking to get involved in this?"

Despite my success in college and my Ph.D., self-doubt had been my companion since I was a young boy; it didn't give in easily. Even thoughts of one of my favorite Robert Browning quotes that rests behind a picture frame in my office—"Ah, but a man's reach should exceed his grasp"—failed to diffuse the growing feelings of anxiety that were rising from the pit of my stomach. As an adult, I had amassed a bag full of tricks to make these inner enemies go away. Usually they worked; today was an exception. As I walked along, it felt like the calm before the storm.

Sweaty palms made even opening the door to the conference room a chore. It was an intimate setting, with twelve chairs around two conference tables. An aisle divided the chairs, with a podium at the front and a marker board in back. Beautiful pictures of children outlined the classroom. As I often did when I was working with peers, I chose a seat in the back of the room, opposite the podium.

Several minutes later, three participants joined me. As I quietly tried to calm my nerves, the woman to my left observed, "I guess you'll be the recorder this morning." "Excuse me?" I exclaimed. She continued, "The person sitting closest to the marker board gets to be the secretary."

Now, the anxiety that had been slowly building burst forth like an erupting volcano. My Ph.D. and the fact that I was a presenter for the third week provided little peace of mind as my heartbeat raced. Little yawns became more frequent, masking my growing need for oxygen. "No way!" I thought. And, instantaneously I was back in the third grade, vividly feeling the fear of misspelling words in front of the class, worrying about my performance. I could not risk the humiliation and embarrassment of even one misspelled word back then. Thirty plus years later it wasn't much different. I had to move, do something to relieve the mounting tension, frustration, and anxiety.

"O.K. Mark, think of a reason for moving that makes sense to the three people sitting here." That was it; that was all I had to do. I had become adept at acting smart while feeling dumb. I delivered my line casually, hiding the anxiety.

"I'm going to have a hard time staying awake with the sun beating down on the back of me if I stay this close to the window."

Fortunately, it made sense to the person who had pronounced my role as record keeper. She exclaimed, "That's a great idea. I believe I will move over as well." As if my strategy was not good enough, I continued, "I guess I could move the marker board next to me." It was a calculated risk. I presumed there would be little interest in such a trite comment; I was right. The others maintained their silence and the marker board remained in its original place.

I breathed a heavy sigh of relief. Their silence was the key that unlocked the massive ball and chain that had taken hold of me. No longer would I be record keeper, experiencing each moment of that seminar as a precarious balance between success and failure. I could breathe again. My secret was safe.

The experience at the small private college suggested that the coming-out party was incomplete. I never pursued any task that revealed too much inferiority. I also never pursued any task without preparation. If I wasn't prepared, I learned how to refuse in a firm, but polite manner. I became adept at good excuses that would get me off the hook. They filled my secret magic bag. For instance, when a faculty member once used my lack of seniority as a reason for having me take meeting notes, I quickly retorted, "Have you seen my handwriting? Trust me, you don't want me taking notes. I would be glad to lead the discussion if someone else can write more legibly." This approach worked more than once.

When asked at church to read scriptures, I was too weak to brave the chance of making a mistake reading aloud. I simply said I was not familiar enough with the passage to read it. Offending someone became less of an evil than making a mistake. Another time, I was asked to bless the food at the beginning of a luncheon. I remember the feeling of resolve; the instantaneous beads of sweat collecting on my brow. I responded without wit or humor, saying very respectfully, "There must be many other people who are used to blessing the food; I am not one of them." The gentleman left me alone with no second thoughts; I left feeling inadequate. I could easily have done this had I written a prayer beforehand; however, I was not inclined to set myself up for embarrassment. Spontaneity was not part of my repertoire.

My personal life was no different. When my wife, Linda and I were at parties or with friends, I would not come close to a game of *Trivial Pursuit* for fear of not being able to answer a basic question. I became supersensitive to issues that reflected my inabilities. I was opposed to my wife talking with the car mechanic about our car troubles, or with the person at the hardware store about our leaky faucet. That was male territory, my responsibility. Yet, I didn't know the first thing about such matters. Looking smart; it was my own personal Holy Grail, my lifelong quest.

My all-consuming desire to keep my real-self secret from the world forced me to take fewer risks in life than other people usually do. Yet, looking back, I know that I've taken many risks. I didn't succumb entirely to the pressure of my sense of vulnerability. Nevertheless, over the years, it caused me to don layer after layer of protection, in the end becoming someone I hardly recognized.

It was during this time that the closet door cracked and I began stepping out to talk with audiences about my personal story. I went public for one reason—my desire to effect change among adults who influenced struggling learners. Having grown up facing the daily challenges a learning disability presents, I wanted to help ease the burden for other children experiencing similar despair. I had received tenure in my job, so a protective shield of sorts was covering my professional career. Most of all, I was feeling a deep-seated desire to know and be myself. The yearning had been bubbling in my consciousness since I completed my Ph.D. It was the one journey that could bring the light of understanding to all of the many challenges I had faced. It was the road less traveled, but also the road to freedom.

The turning point came during a weekend seminar that my wife and I attended, hosted by Dennis and Rita Bennett, (1971) authors of *The Holy Spirit and You*. They shared twelve common experiences that typically resulted in the need for people to seek inner healing. The last experience involved people who had grown up with learning disabilities. I tried to keep the shock from being too obvious. Linda and I discussed whether I should spend some private time with two prayer partners who would help me explore this area. Initially, I discounted the need to do so, but Linda gently urged me on: "Why don't you just try it and see what happens?" I did, and my life was forever changed. For the first time, I realized how much time I had spent, since I was a very young child, trying to scrape away the part of me that reflected my learning disabilities experiences. I wept for a long time. The emotional release was unfathomable as my inner demons were wrestled, one by one, to their defeat.

During the rest of the seminar, I was exposed to the idea that God embraced all of me, including my disabilities. It became an unbelievably potent personal revelation, and propelled me to a more open attitude about myself. I learned the importance of embracing 100 percent of me, without conditions and apologies. I learned that I did not need cleansing. Most important, I realized that my life was designed to champion this cause on behalf of others.

I began presiding as president of the Beaumont Learning Disabilities Association and continued in that capacity for several years. I began to use my childhood experiences as a launching pad to champion the cause for children and adolescents with learning problems. I began writing editorials for the newspaper as well as a "Dr. Mark" column for the Beaumont Learning Disability newsletter, sharing some of the ideas and strategies that were the precursors of this book. I talked about "mailclerkitis," the unjust categorization of children. I wrote about the "hero/goat syndrome," wherein some children receive better treatment at the expense of others. I offered new ways of thinking and acting that conveyed a more unconditional relationship between parent and child or teacher and student. Some people embraced my ideas; others were threatened to the core. The experience was freeing for me. As my ideas grew, so did my desire to become a greater force in effecting change in the world of children and adolescents with learning disabilities.

This does not mean that thoughts and feelings of self-consciousness have been eliminated from my life. Far from it! However, my reframed thoughts now dominate those that say, "You are not smart enough." I still become defensive about things I don't know. I'm not always an open book. I still wonder about people's perceptions of my "smarts." I still walk around with a protective shield, but it's not as thick as before, nor do I wear it as often.

I have become impassioned in my speaking engagements; fighting for the rights of children with learning challenges, fighting against the stereotypes that permeate our lives and our school environments. There are many people who strive to elevate themselves at the expense of others. While they may not be able to rise above others through their own accomplishments, they do so by lowering the status of others. These are the bullies of our schools, some in sheep's clothing. They are also the bullies of our adult lives, many of whom capture fame and fortune along the way.

Going public as a person with learning disabilities has given my life a new meaning and purpose. People whose eyes betray their competent exterior frequently corner me after my presentations. I remember one gentleman, tears streaming down his face, sadly profess, "You cannot imagine how often I hide my problems. It is the biggest and darkest secret in my life." Others hear my words as permission to give up their struggle to hide. A very successful businessman recounted the many ways he had ridiculed others because of their mistakes, in order to hide his own. The majority of the people talk about their own secrets, their true selves that parents, teachers, even friends knew little about. Most people who hear me speak realize, as did I, that the very part of themselves they have disliked and hidden to the world for so long is the very part of themselves that contributed to their success. For them, and for me, acceptance has been a physical, emotional, and spiritual healing process.

Today, it is not enough for me to participate only in my own coming-out party. I want children who grow up challenged to have their own party. The mental messages in Chapter Three, the injustices described in Chapter Four, and the strategies outlined in Chapter Five are all designed to prepare parents, teachers, and children for the celebration.

For every party we must send out invitations. What follows is my expression of interest in children and adults touched by the challenges of learning:

Dear Friends,

I want you to know of my concern when you face the challenges of learning differences, especially when you have little support to guide you. I long for you to have the same opportunities as others. These include laughing, running, and talking face-to-face with others, rather than being mocked, chased, and talked about by them. I know the pain and suffering that you feel. There is no magic cure to protect us against the behaviors by adults and peers that result in these feelings.

But, take heart! There is insulation that can protect us against crumbling under such hurt and suffering. That insulation is never but a thought away. Our thoughts become our most powerful tool, our most potent weapon. We can climb steep mountains, walk through briar-soaked valleys, and swim through mighty currents with a belief that says, "I can and I will."

There will always be a chorus of detractors favoring quitting, but there can also be a chorus of supporters encouraging succeeding. My hope and dream is that you access that support through the exercise of your head, heart, and hand. Use your head to think positive thoughts, your heart to embrace those thoughts, and your hands to take action. You will always be as strong as your insistence allows. There is no man or woman, girl or boy alive who can say, "I have no weaknesses or disabilities." There is also no man or woman, girl or boy who fails to have strengths and abilities. We each have more of one or less of the other. That is the truth. Plain and simple.

Another truth is that everyone has the ability to succeed. Make this your guiding light. Don't fall prey to a fear of your own shortcomings. Don't fall prey to those who fail to recognize your strengths. I will not let their actions cause me to reject my I CAN thinking. I will sketch into my mind not only my hopes and dreams, but also an insistence that I can fulfill those hopes and dreams. In this pursuit, listen to those internal messages that reinforce the fortitude to keep trying, a willingness to delay achievement, and an acceptance of any outcome that reflects your very best.

Seek your own happiness, rather than the happiness prescribed by so many others. In doing so, you may resist the unhappiness fallen upon the many. I hope to prepare you now with peace of mind, a heart full of self-appreciation, and the desire to withstand the storms, for life will present you with storms all along the way. Go forth with a mighty team, lead by your mighty thoughts designed to filter the negative and feed the positive. Know that you can succeed. That is the truth and the truth shall set you free.

It is time for parents, educators and others who work with individuals with learning disabilities to exercise the thoughts that will help children experience success and realize their dreams. *Bound and Determined* contains messages and strategies to guide parents and teachers through that process. Those of you who take up this quest will experience joy and fulfillment beyond what you thought possible. Yes, it is a treacherous jungle, but you will enter it aware of the pitfalls and snares, and armed with ideas that can transform the jungle into a tropical oasis for children with learning challenges. Look into the eyes of the children you meet along the way. Take their hands; be their guides. The difference you make in their lives will not go unnoticed. God speed.

CHAPTER THREE

DR. MARK'S MENTAL MESSAGES FOR SUCCESS

Thoughts breed feelings; feelings breed actions; actions breed character; character breeds destiny. Our destiny is just a thought away!

esse came to see me about his son's plummeting grades. As he started talking, I noticed the signs of defeat written all over him—slumped shoulders, head bent, sleepy eyes, weak voice, and a very tentative attempt to communicate. "I don't know where to begin," he murmured. Still, the fact that Jesse had reached out to me and was willing to try reflected an inner strength not supported by his outer appearance. Jesse continued with a deep and heavy sigh. "I always hoped my son would not follow in my footsteps. But apparently, he has." There was now only despair in his voice; he even seemed disturbed by the thought. I gently probed, "What is so bad about your footsteps?" Urgently his eyes met mine with a bewildered, almost apologetic look, as if to say, "Can't you tell? Don't you know?" Trying to hide his embarrassment, Jesse elaborated: "I knew when I was a little boy that I wouldn't amount to anything. Now it seems my son won't either. Like father like son."

Jesse's words were powerful. I sat wondering if he realized just how powerfully those words affected not only his destiny, but that of his son, too. What concerned me more were the mental messages ingrained in Jesse throughout his life—messages of failure, helplessness, and inertia—that were now being unconsciously handed down to his son.

The mind is a tremendous force; it rules our thoughts, communications, and experiences—both good and bad. It is the powerhouse behind our feelings and actions, the background voice that shapes our characters and our destinies. While it can be a source of inspiration and hope, it is often a fertile breeding ground for insecurities, doubts, and fear. It is a mental battlefield where the war between personal good and evil takes place on a daily basis throughout our lives. Most of us learn the rules of engagement and become victorious through practice, our minds becoming strong and trusted allies. For children with learning disabilities, the opposite is too often the case.

How can we help our children fight this war and give them the armor and resolve they need to attain success in their lives? For many of us, it involves a new way of thinking. For me, it also involved learning to combine skill with will and a strong desire to succeed. A friend once told me, "Mark, the foundation of your destiny will always be the thoughts cultivated in your mind." This friend was a star athlete and at the top of his class. It was not a challenge for him to believe that. But for me, it was almost impossible to even think positively—let alone take positive action—when my world was filled with daily academic challenges, student innuendoes, teachers' disappointments and my own mental demons.

Fortunately, other adults recognized my plight and came to the rescue in various ways. They encouraged me to reframe my thinking and look at the world through a new set of lenses. By concentrating on my positive qualities, they helped me gain perspective about the shortcomings. Their encouragement and the lessons learned over the years evolved into the Dr. Mark Messages.

I cannot think of too many self-help messages that contributed more to my forward progress than the ones reflected here. These "mental messages" are designed to combat the poisonous statements, events, or experiences that everyone faces from time to time, but that are a daily occurrence in the lives of children with learning challenges.

Too little attention is paid in our culture today to helping our children understand that the words they quietly whisper to themselves influence their feelings, actions, character, and destiny. Each Dr. Mark Message helps pave the way for the mind to recognize and accept more of the positive thoughts that ultimately affect the destinies of the children who hear them. Collectively, they are messages designed to help parents and teachers create a path of potential and prosperity for children with learning challenges. Some of the messages focus on reforming the thoughts of adults, while others assist parents and/or teachers in reframing children's thoughts. Just as physical muscles become soft, unreliable, and unable to withstand obstacles unless exercised, so do mental muscles atrophy without regular and consistent use. My goal is to encourage parents and teachers to help children develop strength of character—toughness—to fight the obstacles that will, undoubtedly, come their way. This toughness must be more than skin-deep. It must penetrate through the mind to the very core of their being, infusing their hearts, souls, and spirits with a resolve to face their challenges and keep on trying.

Discuss the Dr. Mark Messages in the home or in school environments. They need to be visible and referred to continuously. Make them into a poster, write them on a corner of the blackboard, or tape them to the children's desks. Use them as guidelines when communicating and interacting with children challenged with learning problems.

The mental message playing over and over in Jesse's mind was, "I will never achieve." And, he didn't! When he came to see me, he had already adopted a new mental message: "My son will never achieve." Undoubtedly, his son was already hearing that silent voice in his own mind—learning challenges do that.

The mental messages are designed to help children replace their negative "self-talk" with positive thoughts. We must help them revise their script that says, "I want to quit" to one that says, "I have just begun to fight." This help often requires that adults also change their script from one that says, "My child will not achieve," to one that says, "My child not only can achieve but my child will achieve." This script-changing strategy is wonderfully articulated in Brooks and Goldstein's (2004) chapter, "Changing the Words of Life." They outline seven steps for changing the negative scripts voiced by the Jesses of our world. As the authors rightfully suggested, changing scripts is formidable. Equally accurate, it is essential.

MENTAL MESSAGE #1
How fast you develop doesn't determine how far you can succeed.

I remember a five-year-old boy named Abraham, who always raised his hand when I asked a question. His excitement was contagious as he furiously waved his arms, his body screaming out, "Ask me, ask me, ask me!" Every expression communicated confidence. "I know, I know," he would yell. The fact was, he rarely did. He had a severe speech impediment that challenged his learning, and most of his responses took rabbit trails out to left field. However, that didn't discourage Abraham; he believed in himself.

Abraham reminded me of the story about the tortoise and the hare. The hare, with his speed and agility, was lured into a false sense of accomplishment. As a result, it was the tortoise, even with his slow pace, who won the race. All around Abraham, his peers were surpassing his academic development. They assimilated new information with ease, and spent their free time relaxing in enjoyable pursuits. Abraham was like the tortoise, working very hard as he slowly plodded along, but never taking his eyes off the finish line. What helped Abraham?

Abraham's parents and teacher believed in him and in his ability to succeed. Furthermore, they acted in a manner consistent with that belief. They refused the "mindset" that Abraham could not perform because of his slow pace. They celebrated his enthusiasm, encouraged him to keep trying, and disregarded the self-defining academic "measurements"—the standardized examinations, attitudes, and predispositions. The result? Fifteen years later, Abraham excelled through college while some of the "hares" in his class never made it out of high school.

Of course, success is not exclusively dependent upon how children do in school. Brooks and Goldstein (2004) are right to remind us that success can encompass such features as positive relationships with others, contentment in a variety of roles, and a feeling of optimism. Unfortunately, this present age of academic accountability does little to encourage children like Abraham to feel contentment without measuring up academically. It is hard for the Abraham's to feel a sense of optimism when their names are left off the A/B honor rolls published down the corridors of school hallways.

When adults refuse to measure success by speed, children learn to keep trying with less worry. This is a message helpful for adults and children alike.

MENTAL MESSAGE #2
It doesn't take being at the top of your class to be successful.

Charlotte arrived home from middle school looking bewildered. "Dad, what's wrong with the other students down the hall from my class?" Her question made little sense to me. With an equally bewildered look, I asked for clarification. Her response was telling: "The teachers always say that the students in my class are the cream of the crop and that the future of our world depends on us."

Her response, and the accompanying sentiment, was hard to swallow, considering my son was one of those students "down the hall." Also, as a teacher prone to rebellious thought, I resisted the mindset that children outside the gifted and talented class, and especially children demonstrating learning problems, could not contribute to the future of our nation. It just wasn't true! It also minimized the importance for maximizing learning for all students.

There is a bill of goods that some school systems are still selling, that has no place in the classroom. It says that only the "smart" kids ever amount to anything. Many youngsters are taught that the students at the top of the class are guaranteed the enviable position of not only being successful in school, but also becoming successful beyond school. This is done overtly, as in my daughter's class or covertly, through off-handed comments, selective praise, or administrative emphasis. Sadly, this is one of the most marketed, yet worthless, pieces of merchandise we sell. It's time to replace it with a new mental message, one that acknowledges what is already occurring: people do graduate without honors and become successful and *are* part of the cream that rises to the top. This can be observed in the hundreds of thousands of distinguished teachers, carpenters, doctors, lawyers, plumbers, engineers, electricians, business people, as well as homemakers who struggled with their performance during childhood. There are thousands of CEOs of major corporations who depend on their secretaries to correct their spelling, proof their grammar, and pull out the important points from a report.

A more vivid example of such exceptionality was introduced through a man who remodeled our bathroom. The job required completion of numerous complex tasks such as the removal of a wall and window, the change in placement of the toilet and sink, the installation of a handicap accessible shower, the correction of plumbing and the wiring of a new light fixture. During the first few days, our communication consisted of written messages. My wife's consternation grew, as those messages appeared to be ignored. On one particular day, we left a note that read, "Mike, please lock the gate behind you." We arrived home from work to experience more frustration. The gate was unlocked, leaving a backyard pool accessible to neighborhood children. It was then that the meaning of the trail of missed messages became all too apparent. The genius, who could cut and place tile with absolute precision, could not read. I was saddened at how slow we were to process the many signs and symptoms that cried, "Spare me the print!" This thirty plus year old man was good. He was good at dodging the print rich world that hid his disabilities. Fortunately, he discovered a way to keep his wonderful abilities in the forefront continually placing his weaknesses in the shadows of his strengths. I remember lamenting to my wife, "Isn't it too bad that one must work so hard to hide his challenges? A better world would be a world that teaches, I can embrace with pride my disabilities and abilities." That way, he could more freely say, "Cooper's, there is very little I can't remodel, but I will need oral instructions rather than written instructions. Reading is not my forte."

God's exhortation that in my weakness, then I am made strong became especially meaningful for me during my Ph.D. program. There were times when I didn't think I could make it through my program because of mental weaknesses. Even worse, I shared my program chairman, Dr. Walter Hodges, with one of the sharpest candidates in our class. I constantly compared myself to him. I was ever so conscious of our differences. He was, by far, a better student than I. Of course, he would amount to more than I would. It took several years to realize the enormous impact that way of thinking had on my progress through my Ph.D. program—the mental toll, the energy that it sucked from me—energy that could have been better applied to my own success!

Our kids are constantly being compared to one another. Unfortunately, some are often being told they don't measure up. Thousands of school districts in the United States separate students into gifted and talented classes. Few children with learning disabilities make it into these classrooms; they don't "learn right" to qualify. Conversely, we pull difficult or challenged students out into special education classes or resource classes, reinforcing the theme that they are being grouped because of their shared inadequacies, their deficiencies, their shortcomings. We ingrain a negative message in these children, "You're not smart enough to qualify, you don't measure up." It's no wonder they don't. We teach them not to.

It's time to replace these negative images with a way of thinking that celebrates achievements and promotes positive mental messages. I know from experience that being at the top of the class does not make a person successful. I also learned that being nearer to the bottom of the class does not make a person unsuccessful. It was an essential lesson for me to learn.

As I shared some of my personal experiences with my daughter, that day, she learned important mental messages too: all children have the potential to contribute to our world, and success isn't defined by just academic test scores and rank in a classroom. More important, she learned not to quickly judge one classmate as capable and another as incapable. Charlotte learned fortune telling should remain in the fortune cookies and be treated skeptically whenever communicated. Further, she learned that the cream that rises to the top might come in a variety of flavors—contentment, athleticism, or good relational skills. In other words, children who demonstrate "smarts" as it relates to people, music, art, bodily-kinesthetics, word, and/or logic might very well distinguish themselves as adults. Smart comes in all sorts and sizes. There is no one-smart-fits-all category of success.

When adults believe children can succeed, regardless of where they fall in the academic line-up, they prepare fertile ground for success among many rather than a chosen few.

MENTAL MESSAGE #3
I am as good as "we" are.

It takes a number of "them" merging into one perfect whole. Few people accomplish much single-handedly. Without the strong support of my mother and several other mentors along the way, I would not have accomplished as much as I did. However, it wasn't always an easy road, or one that I immediately wanted to follow.

Children today need to learn how to interact with teachers and parents in order to receive extra help. Peers can be an invaluable source of assistance, but children must first learn that seeking help is a sign of courage rather than a sign of weakness. Adopting this mental message is easier said than done. As children grow, they seek to try things out on their own. A developmental feature of adolescence involves the propensity to individuate—adolescents want to depend on others less and less. Adolescents do not want the help they often need. This is even truer for children with learning disabilities. Nevertheless, the help is exactly what they need to fulfill their many hopes and dreams.

There's a fine line between knowing when to ask for help and when to persevere independently. Children with learning disabilities often spend so much of their time buried in just trying to stay afloat academically that they don't recognize the life preservers that are around them in the form of outside assistance. Parents, teachers, and children need a mindset that interdependence, rather than independence, has the greater value. We must help them reframe their thinking and apply the thought, "Separate, we are weak! United, we stand strong." This mental message not only encourages action, it gives the team permission to lean on one another. Also, children want to see themselves as brave, courageous, and bold. Children can learn that a proactive position utilizing resources is a reflection of bravery and a cherished virtue.

Tisha had seen numerous counselors about her rebelliousness toward her mom, the family member prone to help Tisha with schoolwork. Tisha came to my office very defensive, understandable considering her learning problems. "I don't need any help!" she protested with her arms folded across her chest and a sour and defiant facial expression. When it came to schoolwork, mom dictated and Tisha resisted. The dynamics of the relationship were failing them both, and neither of them could see the other as part of the same team.

An important part of our counseling session involved reframing their mindsets and introducing the mental message, "I am as good as we are." Once the mom began to see her daughter as someone to empower rather than victimize, Tisha began to see herself as an advocate for her success and able to contribute greatly to the solution. Tisha began to individuate while learning how to engage others in her pursuit of success. An amusing statement made by Tisha several weeks into this mind-altering experience revealed the new approach she had adopted: "Mom, it looks like I'm the president of the board and you're a board member. And by the way, Mom, you're a top-notch board member and cheap at that." By changing their mental messages from being rooted in dissension to being rooted in collaboration, cooperation, and personal empowerment, they both succeeded and their relationship improved greatly, as did Tisha's schoolwork. It came as no surprise when Tisha remarked to her mom: "I think the time has come for the president of this company to get a raise."

When teachers, parents, and children with learning problems treat the whole as greater than the sum of its parts, they begin to maximize the importance of the team.

MENTAL MESSAGE #4
You can't fail, if you don't quit.

This is a message for adults and children alike. Each of us experiences failure from time to time throughout our lives. It might be a strikeout at the plate, a low test score, hitting the wrong note on the keyboard, losing a sale, or failing to find employment. But most of us experience successes too that help keep our perspective balanced. This is often not the case for children and adults with learning disabilities, who consequently find it difficult to separate defeat from failure.

Parents, teachers, and children with learning disabilities must learn to taste defeat without feeling the pangs of failure and know the difference between the two. Defeat must be placed into a proper perspective: No one is exempt from defeat. But defeat is nothing more than a setback, a mini-loss. While the setback may require change, the change can nevertheless represent forward progress.

Failure, on the other hand, is terminal. It occurs when someone quits, when forward motion ceases altogether. Imbedded in failure is not only the expression "I can't," but also "I am unwilling to keep trying."

Many men and women who have accomplished great things taste defeat on a regular basis. Famous football quarterbacks like Joe Montana, Dan Marino, and John Elway have thrown thousands of interceptions in their career. Olympic gold medalists in gymnastics fall hundreds of times during practices and sometimes during Olympic performances. Defeat is nothing but an opportunity to learn. It is a required step to something much better. Defeat strengthens our resolve and makes many men and women invincible. Few adults or children would oppose attaining that degree of success. This can happen when we encourage the mindset that views our defeats as opportunities for course corrections, rather than as roadblocks along the way.

In college, I was defeated by freshmen English. Rather than accepting the "F" as a symbol of failure, I chose to view the "F" as faltering—I faltered. I reframed my thinking, even allowing for a forgiveness clause. This view helped me recover from my disappointment and move forward.

While I have chosen to use this forgiving mindset as one that propels children forward in the midst of challenges, Brooks and Goldstein (2004) provided a very thorough and incisive look at the power of resilience. It is through children's power of resilience that they can face adversity successfully. As the authors indicated, a resilient mindset does not imply that one is free from stress, pressure, and conflict, but rather that one can successfully cope with problems as they arise.

Parents, teachers, and children need to embrace a more forgiving mindset, where faltering is allowed without inappropriate retribution from self or others. In so doing, the message of despair can be replaced with the message of disappointment. The latter is far more forgiving.

MENTAL MESSAGE #5
Make willpower a #1 priority.

I learned a tremendous lesson when my father, a man whose type-A personality never said, "stop" suddenly had a heart attack. Dad left a grocery store with a bag of groceries in hand. But he didn't get far before his six-foot-six-inch, 300 pound frame slammed to the concrete near the car. Packages were strewn everywhere as he lay perfectly still without pulse or respiration. A gentleman was first to approach while several others began to encircle with terrified and very confused looks. One person cried, "Isn't there anyone who can do something?" as the minutes passed and they stood there watching Dad's skin color become increasingly gray. Finally, six minutes into this tragedy one of Dad's nurse practitioners noticed the commotion. Pushing her way through the crowd, she administered CPR and mouth-to-mouth resuscitation to revive her professor. But the six minutes without assistance caused irreparable damage and Dad died after languishing for about three months.

Angry, I asked the typical question, "Why has such a fate befallen such a great pediatrician whose record of saving lives was tremendous?" Over time a transformation occurred in my thinking, going from very negative to very positive. I began to ask a new question, "Why did several adults ignore a fellow human being's life-threatening need for CPR while standing just a few feet away?" I spent endless hours pondering this question. Was it their lack of knowledge? No, most people have a basic understanding of CPR and/or mouth-to-mouth resuscitation, if not its exact science. What was missing? What was it that separated a person who would have helped dad from those who merely stood by watching?

The question awakened me during the early hours of many mornings until one particular morning. I remembered reading an article written by Lilian Katz (1992), a leading expert in child development, about components of learning. Disposition, desire, and attitude came to mind as the defining reasons that propel people to action. Knowledge and skills are necessary but not sufficient in many circumstances. The adults standing around Dad that day had the knowledge and skills to help. They lacked the will to apply them.

Just as God transforms tragedy into opportunity, I began to connect this lesson to children. Lilian Katz (1992) helped me capture the missing link. Katz insisted that much time is devoted to building knowledge and enhancing skills. Less time is devoted to fostering dispositions. Dispositions, according to Katz (1993), are tendencies to exhibit frequently, consciously, and voluntarily a pattern of behavior that is directed to a broad goal. Dispositions include desire and willpower. Cantor (1990) pointed out that just because people have the knowledge about something and the skill to do something does not mean they do it. For instance, children who have the skills to read and write may not have a desire to read and write. The most elaborate, creative behavior modification system failed to entice me to read and write. Why? It was not fun. In fact, it was torturous. This is not uncommon among struggling learners.

Children with learning problems are expected to expend tremendous energy and effort building their knowledge and enhancing their skills. Parents and educators teach and re-teach, trying to help these children survive in the academic arenas. In many instances, most of the effort is focused on outward academic achievements: "Why don't you remember that answer?" "You are not trying hard enough." "We are going to sit here all day or all night, if necessary, until you learn the spelling words." Children can easily become discouraged over the emphasis we, as a society, place on knowledge building and skill development.

The struggling learners "will" to build such knowledge and enhance such skills cannot be ignored.

One of the great and most expensive tragedies in our society involves the thousands of adolescents with learning disabilities who become juvenile delinquents. I strongly believe most of these kids have the skill to succeed. Somewhere along the way they lost the disposition or will to keep trying. Life became such a wreck that other, more rebellious, behaviors seemed easier and more attractive options.

If we are serious about helping our children achieve success, we need to add another ingredient to the knowledge plus skills equation: Our children need the disposition, "willpower." They need the willpower to *apply* the skill power. We are adept at emphasizing the lessons, the objectives, and academics. In our efforts we have sorely neglected teaching children about desire or the "want to." This is especially important among children who struggle with assignments that emphasize their weaknesses.

What can parents and teachers do? They must celebrate the teaching of willpower just like they celebrate teaching of science and math concepts. That is, they must celebrate the teaching of willpower alongside learning to spell words, calculate math facts, or write a main idea. We consistently applaud children's accomplishments when they learn bodies of knowledge and sets of skills. We must give equally thunderous applause when children demonstrate willpower—regardless of the immediate academic outcome.

Katz (1992) outlined five strategies for promoting dispositions, such as willpower. First, resist teaching concepts before children are ready. It is hard for children to have the "want to" disposition when the expectations are unreasonable. Second, ensure that the skills are obtainable before the dispositions are expected. Hope is often defined as the desire with the expectation to obtain what is desired. False hope is little fuel for willpower. It is often important for children's efforts to be reinforced. The disposition to read is frequently dependent upon children's skills to read. Third, provide environmental conditions conducive to disposition development. For example, children thrive on confidence. Activities and requirements that humiliate and embarrass become conditions that weaken or perhaps diminish dispositions, such as confidence in self. Rogoff, Gauvain, and Ellis (1990) recommended scaffolding techniques designed to support the learning of dispositions. Confidence can be learned when struggling learners experience success. Often, this success must come in very small increments. Fourth, more formalized activities and experiences can be organized to teach dispositions. Mario was a fifth-grade struggling learner who expressed tremendous frustration over his reading problems. In the course of one conversation, I commented, "Mario, frustration will follow you for grades to come. It is important to learn how to handle such frustration." Several minutes passed before Mario returned to that statement with resolve. He challenged, "Dr. Mark, I didn't like what you said about frustration following me." I asked what bothered him about that. He exclaimed, "I don't like to be frustrated!" Coping with frustration will be an important catalyst for Mario's growth. It must be taught with the same vengeance as it is felt. Finally, dispositions are best taught through modeling. Mario must see his parents and teachers face frustration successfully. Coping with frustration can be neither a hidden part of a teacher's curriculum nor a parent's agenda.

There is far too little fanfare within the wall of academia over this important mindset. It is will, not skill, that propels children into study, practice, persistence, and perseverance. It is children's willpower that makes, or breaks, their spirits and, subsequently, their futures. The development of this disposition becomes a powerful milestone along the road toward success.

Children are far more prone to develop knowledge and exercise skills once they have embraced the mindset that says, "Try, and if all things appear to fail, try again!"

MENTAL MESSAGE #6
Don't cap children's capabilities by the label, "overachievement."

Overachievement is a buzzword these days in the school environment. Parents and teachers use it liberally when faced with a surprise success or children's unexpected achievement. It's as though we plan for mediocrity or worse, failure, and then label success as overachievement! But who are the overachievers? Are they the children who have accomplished more than expected? If so, isn't that preposterous? Aren't we just capping children's capabilities when we label their efforts as overachievement?

The real danger here lies in the perceptions children gradually adopt. They begin applying the same mindset with little prompting. How often have you heard one student say to another: "Wow, I got an 86. I guess I was lucky or maybe the test was just easy." Think about it! Children accomplish an assignment, perform masterfully on an exam, or conduct an imaginative experiment and what happens? They receive little credit from self or others when overachievement is used to explain their success. The overachievement message undermines and sabotages the notion that effort had much to do with their performance. Instead, when we emphasize effort rather than ability, children understand that effort correlates with success.

Many children with learning problems are underachievers rather than overachievers. They are achievers who have yet to grow up and demonstrate their capabilities, regardless of their age. Many years ago, Flip Wilson, a comedian and the host of a variety show on television, used to say, "What you see is what you get!" This is not true for many children with learning problems. I say, on behalf of these children that "What you see is not what you get, because what I got I haven't shown you yet!" Adults must believe in the hidden talents and skills that children with learning problems have yet to demonstrate. Otherwise, they limit the very achievement they claim to want. Parents and teachers must encourage children with learning problems to uncover and reveal these abilities, and know that beneath their every effort there is more waiting to surface.

Su Lin was a perfect example of the problem of using the overachievement label too liberally. The sixteen-year-old sat in my office while listening to her mom explain, "My daughter is doing the very best she can. I suspect she will always be a C student. Occasionally, she gets an A or B, but I believe that reflects overachievement." This proclamation aggravated Su Lin, as well it should. While her mom was out of the office, she explained, "C grades are normal for me and A's are abnormal. Mom has never given me credit for making anything above a C. I guess I'm not supposed to," I reflected, "You are not supposed to?" The young girl continued, "When I make better grades, my mom and my teachers tell me I'm overachieving." I then asked, "What do you mean by overachievement?" She retorted, "Overachievement means that I really don't have the ability to perform at the level I am performing." I challenged, "Does that make sense to you? You just accomplished something. Yet, the something you accomplished doesn't count for much because you shouldn't be able to do what you're doing."

While it was a mouthful to consider, Su Lin began to understand the negative mental message that overachievement conveyed. Once she and her mom reframed their thinking about overachievement, they began to give credit where credit was due. As a result, they associated Su Lin's good performance with her effort, the one thing that Su Lin could control. This was far better than Su Lin attributing her accomplishment to things she could not control—ability, luck, or lack of task difficulty.

Removing the "over" and concentrating on the "achievement" opens the door for children with learning challenges to surpass their expectations for success in life.

MENTAL MESSAGE #7
Understanding requires no patience.

Nikista and his parents were like boxers in their separate corners of the ring during their first visit. Their agitation was obvious, and little communication occurred between them. Each side sat poised, waiting for me to ring the bell for the next bout.

Round 1: The parents threw the first punch. "Forgetful, irresponsible, unmotivated, and disorganized, that's Nikista!" Not surprisingly, Nikista quickly countered as if he just got sucker-punched, "I can't do anything right. No matter what I do, you complain. I don't care what you say anyway." Despite his words, it was obvious to me that Nikista did care. He also seemed to need the safe environment with me as referee to finally speak his peace without his parents coming unglued.

There was little patience within Nikista's household, and unfortunately for him, his classroom environment was similar. Nikita's teacher was a perfect example of the intricate way in which true understanding and patience are linked. She knew Nikista well. At least, Mrs. Grimes thought she knew Nikista well. She described Nikista as a child who had ability but who did not care. "He is lazy, unmotivated, and does not try to keep up with things. In fact, he rarely completes his homework. It never fails. He will finish the first ten problems and leave the rest blank. Of course, he makes poor grades." Before Mrs. Grimes took her next breath, she complained, "I am losing all my patience with that young man. I just don't know what to do."

Raising a child with learning disabilities is not easy. We all talk about the patience it requires, as though it is a medal we earn by tolerating people who are really "less" in some way. But that is not true! With understanding—true understanding—that is the result of seeing the world through the eyes and minds of the challenged learner, the need for patience dissipates.

Fortunately, Nikista's parents and his teacher began to change once they learned more about Nikista, including his abilities, and understood why he did the things he did. These adults were like horses with blinders on leaving the starting gate, only able to see what was directly in front of them. Their restricted view prevented them from seeing clearly the reasons why Nikista seemed forgetful, disorganized, or unmotivated. It wasn't until I took Nikista and his parents outside and asked the parents to dig a hole with a spoon while Nikista used a shovel that understanding started to surface. It didn't take long for Nikista's dad, whose brow was now soaked in sweat, to say, "I think I get the point."

I wasn't sure if it was sweat or tears falling from his eyes, but I knew he truly understood Nikista's challenges when he finally said, "Nikista has to work harder than many and even then accomplishes less. It must be mighty hard to be Nikista at times." Yes, dad was right. It was hard being Nikista. Their breakthrough in understanding changed how they related to their son from that minute forward. Their understanding required no patience; there was no longer anything to be patient about. They no longer separated into different corners when we talked. They were all on the same team—Nikista as the student and his parents as his trainers.

As a child growing up with a learning disability and later, as an adult who still experienced the aftermath of those tumultuous years, it might come as a surprise to learn that I too had a hard time applying patience to my son, Jim. But, it was so. Looking back, I now know that part of the reason was my lack of true acceptance of who I was, learning disabilities and all. I understood; I had not yet come to accept.

I remember Jim's first-grade teacher exclaiming, "Jim marches to a different drummer" and not being sure if that proclamation was good or bad. He struggled through the first grades of school. The arguments we had about school are forever etched in my mind. "Jim, where is the homework that 'we' did last night? Did you put it in your backpack?" "Jim, where are the books I told you to bring home?" "Jim, why didn't you write down your homework assignments like I told you?" "Jim, why didn't you tell me earlier in the week that you have a history test tomorrow?" I constantly bombarded him with questions, and often with impatience, intolerance, and anger. I was a chip off my dad's block borrowing too little from Mom's example of patience, tolerance, and understanding.

The school wasn't much help either. Jim started to suffer in the fourth grade, as the conflict level intensified with his teacher. While our recent understanding of his challenges helped us, his new teacher continued to display a lack of understanding of children with learning problems. Comments such as, "If Jim were not in my classroom, our classroom standardized scores would average higher," exemplified how unreceptive she was to Jim's challenges.

Who would respond impatiently when inadvertently bumped by a person with a visual impairment? Who would respond impatiently when asked over and over, "Say that again," by a person with a hearing impairment? Certainly, those people do exist and the same is true with "hidden" disabilities. For instance, the secretary at Jim's middle school called my wife at work and to complain that Jim had forgotten to pick up his Ritalin during the lunch hour. The conversation quickly became intense with the secretary demanding, "Your son needs to add responsibility to his life. Kindergartners can remember something as easy as that." One minute later, Linda was on the telephone with me. In tears, she exclaimed, "You need to take care of this problem and stat." The tone of her voice sent a loud signal to me that I had no choice but to leave work immediately and head to our son's school.

Linda was right to believe the secretary was unreasonable in expecting Jim, a child treated for ADD, to consistently remember such a detail. My conversation with the headmaster began offensively: "Your wife is harassing the secretary." Apparently this sole conversation between the secretary and Linda had been enough to constitute harassment. Biting my tongue, I thought, "The less said, the better. Let her vent." The headmaster continued her assault on Linda, citing her unreasonable expectations.

At the end of her diatribe, I quietly asked, "What do you know about the characteristics of children treated for ADD?" Failing to sense her vulnerability, the headmaster confidently began to describe children who manifested disorganization, inattention, and daydreaming. When she added "forgetfulness," she stopped in mid-sentence. Checkmate! Her facial expression changed from confident to apologetic, as she finally made the connection between Jim's challenge and the school's unrealistic expectation. The headmaster quickly solved the problem assuring me that Jim's needs would be met with a greater appreciation for his challenge rather than being seen as an inconvenience to the secretary. What had begun as a very intense problem was solved simply—with understanding. Once the headmaster and secretary understood that Jim was not purposely trying to make their day more miserable, they became teammates prepared to find more creative ways to prompt Jim to remember to get his medication.

Parents and teachers benefit when they incorporate understanding into their thinking. Children with learning problems can make very competent thinking adults feel totally inept. As mentioned, my dad was not a good candidate to help me with schoolwork. Impatient with his own imperfection, each attempt he made to help me spell words accurately challenged his feelings of inadequacy. The result was two people failing—dad and son. Situations like this are not uncommon in our classrooms today, where teachers are often untrained, or sometimes unwilling, to deal with the challenges faced by children with learning disabilities.

Adopting a positive mental message when times are rough goes a long way in helping both the teacher or parent and the child. "I understand the situation enough to apply patience, tolerance, and kindness" is a critical mental message necessary for effective communication among parents, teachers, and children. There will still be good and bad days—regardless of the level of understanding. However, working from a basis of understanding, there will be more good days than bad.

Children with learning problems did not request that God give them their challenges. Adults must learn to accept the children AND their challenges. In so doing, their understanding will breed patience.

MENTAL MESSAGE #8
Beware: Shining too much light on the peaks also illuminates the valleys.

Children with learning problems often experience more emotional valleys than mountain—high experiences. Especially during the school years, they have more opportunities to feel disappointment than excitement. It's a natural tendency for parents and teachers, to spotlight their achievements and shower praise for a job well done. An important message to learn is that each time we draw attention to an accomplishment; we also draw attention to those times when achievement is lacking. Therefore, it becomes important for parents and teachers to understand that a fine line exists between too much and too little praise, and that this varies for each child.

My daughter, Charlotte, once asked, "Dad, do you like me more when I perform?" The question caught me totally off-guard. "What do you mean?" I asked with a bewildered look. Charlotte continued, "Last year I didn't make the Flying Falcon jump rope team and you told me that was O.K. This year when I made the team, you acted like you liked me better." My inquiry grew. "How did I show that?" Charlotte explained that I jumped up and down more, hugged her, and expressed much more excitement. Her comments felt like ice-cold water poured over my head. It awakened me to the message that one positive action can cause a negative reaction.

Prizes, money, and many other kinds of celebrations can communicate to children the message that their worth and sense of self-esteem is dependent upon their performance. Children who become overly excited about their accomplishments can also become hypersensitive to their lack of accomplishments. In many cases, children with learning problems are already disappointed with their lack of accomplishment. It is often an additional, and very stressful burden to contend with the failure to receive a wonderful prize, money, trip to a restaurant, and so on.

One of the great golfers of all times, Jack Nicklaus, was once asked, "Why don't you spend more time talking about your victories?" Jack responded, "I have fewer victories than defeats. If I were to invest much time talking about my victories, I would also be compelled to discuss my defeats. There are more of the latter." For children with learning problems, there are usually more defeats. Great celebrations can often draw more attention to the many defeats than the few victories.

This does not mean that we should not celebrate achievements. Children with learning problems need tremendous encouragement. However, this encouragement does not have to overplay their accomplishments. Our goal should be to help children learn that it is both the peaks and the valleys that contribute to our wholeness as human beings and worthy beings.

Turning down the celebration decimal meter can encourage children with learning problems to see themselves apart from their performance rather than as a compilation of their performances.

MENTAL MESSAGE #9
Never forget the "ability" in disability

"This baby sure does kick a lot!" exclaimed my wife. Her best friend at the time, Rosalyn, responded, "Oh, I just don't see how your baby could be kicking more than mine." The comparisons between the two mothers continued after childbirth. When Linda remarked to Rosalyn that her thirteen-hour childbirth was difficult, Rosalyn's quick reply countered and minimized Linda's claim, "Oh, you can't imagine the difficulty of my childbirth." The comparisons continued during every developmental milestone of their children, always reflecting that one child performed better or earlier than the other. What's important to note is that the emphasis was always on the accomplishment, the ability, as it compared to a suggested deficit or inability in another.

What prayer is common among most expectant parents? Please God make sure my child is healthy. However, just as soon as the child is born, "healthy" is no longer enough. People begin wanting the most beautiful, talented, athletic, and intellectual children.

Children born with learning challenges begin to demonstrate that something is wrong at various stages in their development. Sometimes it occurs before school or once school begins; the fourth grade is a common period for discovery and diagnosis. Up until the discovery, many parents and teachers emphasize the children's abilities and accomplishments. Once children are diagnosed with a learning problem, a new mental message sometimes shifts parents' and teachers' awareness from abilities to inabilities. The children who the day before diagnosis were considered accomplished and capable now become redefined by their exceptions. This redefinition places an entirely different—and often negative—perspective on the treatment of many of these children.

The parents of a sixteen-year-old young man sat down with me to explain the reasons for their teenagers' placement in the hospital for a two-week period. Apparently, the young man experimented with drugs, defied his parents' curfew, ignored his schoolwork, and took liberties with other inappropriate activities. In the course of our conversation, I asked, "What can you tell me that is good about your child?" What are your child's strengths or talents?" Their blank looks conveyed loud and clear they had no clue about their son's positive qualities. I explained that the parents must begin building upon what their son does right rather than wrong. Again, blank looks and then the challenge, "There is nothing that our son does right or positive." I emphasized that the progress we could make in rebuilding a relationship between the parents and their son would depend upon the parents' ability to see the positive and build upon those qualities. I assured them that their son needed to see his strengths, skills, and abilities through their messages.

Teachers and parents of children with learning disabilities must learn to see the abilities in all children, regardless of the label placed upon them. Our prevailing mental message of their learning problems is that children can demonstrate strength regardless of the apparent deficits and can achieve despite the obstacles that may enter their path.

Parents and teachers who exercise this more positive mental message convey to their children the "can do" thinking attitude that propels them to embrace "will do" thoughts.

MENTAL MESSAGE #10
Separate the performer from the performance.

This is one of the most difficult messages to implement in life. It doesn't matter whether the person has disabilities or not. We tend to see people for what they do, not who they are. After all, how many times growing up have you heard the saying, "Actions speak louder than words" or the equally famous refrain, "Do as I say, not as I do."

Joshua was a precocious thirty-three-month-old boy, whose primary problem at preschool was biting. This behavior occurred approximately six times per day. When I asked the director if I could visit the center to observe Joshua, she answered with little hesitation, "Of course, you are welcome to observe the Jeffrey Dahmer of our class." Recalling that Jeffrey Dahmer was a man convicted of many heinous murders, the analogy was disturbing, especially related to someone as young as Joshua. During the visitation, Joshua and two other children caught sight of me. The three children picked up little animal figurines and approached. The intensity in Joshua's eyes was most evident. He pushed a goat toward my face and yelled, "Bite!" As I ignored his pleas for attention and his expression of power, Joshua left only to return with another figurine and the same expression, "Bite!"

Joshua was the product of his performance. Children and adults recognized Joshua as "Joshua the biter." There was no apparent separation between Josh as a person and Josh as a biter in the eyes of the teacher, the students, his parents, or even Joshua himself. This is true with many children challenged by learning problems. The quality of their performance or achievement becomes the measure and description of them as individuals. The kids who often fail become "losers." Those who fall behind with their lessons become "retards." It is no wonder that so many children with learning problems either buckle under the pressure or strive to achieve at all costs.

For most of my life, I felt like the sum total of my performances. Achievement validated me as a person, supported any semblance of high self-esteem, and made me feel a sense of worthiness. As a result, I have spent an inordinate number of years achieving performance labels such as B.S.E., M.S.E., Ph.D., and L.P.C. While my approach has changed over time, it has always been a driving force behind my various accomplishments. This mental mindset carried with it an expensive price tag: lack of self-acceptance, anxiety, fear of failure, and impatience with shortcomings, among others.

It wasn't until later in my life, well after the birth of our son, that I was able to reframe my thinking and start accepting myself and defining myself by different standards. It became a pivotal change in my world and our family.

Children and adults with learning disabilities should be accepted for who they are, rather than what they become through their performances. My son who struggled in school loved the bedtime stories I would tell him about my mistakes, imperfections, and embarrassing moments. "Jim, I can remember a time when I played on an all-star basketball team!" I related one evening. Jim did not seem overly impressed. Then I continued, "At the end of the tournament, the sports commentator announced names of the five most valuable tournament players. Convinced that I would be one, and seeing that the other four were already named, I ran out on the floor expecting to hear my name. Jerry McWilliams, the commenter announced." Jim roared with laughter. He was not the least bit interested in my performance as an all star basketball player. This story reminded him that his dad was a person; more important, that Dad was a person who had imperfections and made mistakes, just as Jim did.

Children with learning problems need teachers and parents who will accept them the way they are. And, don't think you can fool them with half-hearted attempts at acceptance; they can see right though to your heart and know when it's all an act. When we are unconditional in our acceptance and affirmation towards children, their self-esteem blossoms.

Parents and teachers should apply the mental message that conveys to children, "You are the light of my life, and this light shines because of who you are rather than what you have demonstrated." This unconditional appreciation and acceptance can create a contentment that goes beyond any accomplishment.

MENTAL MESSAGE #11
Treat time as your friend rather than your foe.

One of the great tragedies in today's society is our tendency to hurry. Let's guarantee our young children's participation in the most academically geared preschool. Let's make sure our children are able to read, write, and compute earlier and earlier. Increasingly, children are seen acting like and being treated like adults. This hurried child syndrome is causing problems throughout our homes, schools, and communities. We are treating time as our enemy, rather than as our ally.

The hurried child mentality is especially devastating to children with learning disabilities. By the very nature of their learning problem, they need more time! They need extra time to process a question before the next one is asked. They need more time to read without the pressure of time. They need additional time to take exams. And they need time to take smaller steps before a bigger one is required.

It may take me twice as long to accomplish a goal, but once accomplished, it will be more than satisfactory! I have learned to utilize time as my friend. When I sought my doctoral degree, the average stay in the Department of Early Childhood was four years. My stay was longer. To some people, this may have demonstrated a sign of weakness. To me, it demonstrated only that it took longer.

Let others hurry; some of us don't have that luxury, if, indeed, it can be called such. When we accept time as our friend, our goals become attainable, rather than being beyond our reach.

MENTAL MESSAGE #12
You have more to prove to yourself than to others.

Everyone has something to prove. Every day, people try to prove something by the things done or left undone. In my case, it was both. The thing I did the best, I did the most. The thing I did the worst, I did the least. I used sports to prove myself every day while growing through childhood and adolescence. There was not a competition I feared outside the classroom. Athletically, I believed dynamite came in small packages. My four-foot nine-inch frame in the ninth grade reflected such an explosive demeanor. But my physical stature felt more like putty whenever the stage changed from athletic competition to academic pursuits of excellence.

Beyond high school and through my graduate studies, most of my life revolved around the academic arena. My tactics changed. I resorted to leaving things undone where I could stand in the shadows at the right moments hoping to go undetected when academic demonstrations were required. In my secrecy, I was also trying to prove myself. Silence is golden when one leaves the impression of understanding and ability. My actions, reactions, and inactions were designed to help my inabilities, weaknesses, and deficits go undetected. Of course, any and every opportunity to excel was seized, magnified, and broadcast. It was like having a built-in public relations advisor who suggested when to hold the microphone and when to play the part of the ostrich.

Tommy had one of the most sophisticated built-in public relation advisors. At the moment we met, he very confidently challenged, "Where is Libreville on the globe?" I had no clue. Libreville is in Gabon, Africa. Actually, I could not have identified Gabon. Tommy was thrilled by my acknowledgment and continued his charade for the next several weeks. Tommy's need for self-affirmation and self-acceptance bled all over the floor. He was at his best when others thought of him as the best. In this case, he appeared to know the most about cities all over the world.

Tommy met reality when I listened to him continue his shell game with a classmate. Tommy asked his classmate with a confident grin on his face, "How many seats are in the New Orleans Dome?" Without a pause, the classmate exclaimed, "98,653!" The classmate's confidence was no less obvious. Tommy's smile turned as his words softened with, "I knew that, too."

Neither Tommy nor his classmate had any idea about the number of seats in the New Orleans Dome. What they did have was an enormous need to prove themselves to others. I guess it takes one to know one. Tommy and his classmate became buddies, always trying to get the best of the other.

While it is hard for most children and adults to resist trying to prove themselves over and over, it is even harder for children and adults with learning disabilities to resist such a temptation. They see themselves as having much less to give and much more to hide. While this perception may be untrue, it is alive and well in the minds of many struggling learners.

Several years ago, I was talking with a physician friend about an ache in my side. As we talked, he said, "Mark, you need to slow down. You have nothing more to prove. You're successful. You have reached the peak academically. Slow down!" It took me a while to truly understand that I didn't have to compete with such intensity and compulsion any more. It became increasingly apparent there would always be people smarter, richer, and stronger. There will also always be things left undone and new things to do.

Today, I am more relaxed in my endless quest to prove myself. I have realized that whatever I have to prove, I only need to prove to myself, not to others. And therein did most of the stress release its hold on me. I have found I can use that extra energy toward reaching more of my own goals.

Parents and teachers need to help their children gain confidence in life by teaching them to focus more on their own goals, and less on the goals others may set for them. It's often not easy, especially within a society like ours, where such proof is regularly required. Parents and teachers need to provide emergency relief for struggling learners who constantly look outside themselves for the gauge that measures their pursuits and progress. Parents and teachers who use the phrase, "Prove not to me, but prove only to thee," will help raise more confident, courageous, and content children. It will be at this time when those children transcend the boundaries and limitations often set by others.

The real proof of your children's skill is in their ability to follow their own dreams, not the dreams of others.

MENTAL MESSAGE *#13*
Learn to embrace the good, the bad, and the ugly.

Even as an adult, it took me many years to come out of the closet and admit that I had a learning disability. It was my deepest and darkest secret, one that I kept well hidden from friends and colleagues. Once I began excelling academically, I tried to sever any ties with my experiences as a child with a learning problem. In my mind there could be no such thing as a child with a learning problem who received a Ph.D. Subsequently, I disregarded those parts of me that struggled in school, abandoned summer play for reading camp, were tenacious in spirit and exhaustive in details, the parts of me that probably contributed more to my eventual success in life than my triumphs along the way. At first, my childhood experiences felt too bad, too ugly to hold on to. Now, they are too good to let go.

I learned a valuable lesson in trying to separate the good from the bad and the ugly: It can't be done. I had to learn to accept myself unconditionally. Eventually, I embraced the fact that I was a child with a learning disability who grew up to be an adult with a Ph.D. No longer did I regard my childhood experiences only with contempt and my adult experiences with respect. They all took on value and importance in the development of the person I am now. Most important, I learned to convert what I once thought was bad and ugly into something positive and constructive.

Parents and teachers must learn that the whole is always greater than the sum of its parts. In so doing, their children will learn to see themselves as wonderful composites of abilities and disabilities as well as strengths and weaknesses. This will become a catalyst for their pursuit of excellence, happiness, and contentment.

Each of these Dr. Mark's Mental Messages can help parents and teachers frame or reframe their thinking to help their children. Each message is designed to help children at a variety of crossroads in their lives. These messages will not prevent struggling learners from encountering trials and tribulation through their childhood and adult years. They will lessen the intensity of these experiences and enable children to deal more effectively with the roadblocks encountered along the way.

The more common roadblocks children with learning disabilities face are outlined in the next chapter. The roadblocks need to be faced head on, if our children are to reach their full potentials. These injustices, of sorts, are entrenched in our society, as well as in many homes, and school systems. They may never go away, but armed with the wisdom from the Dr. Mark Messages, we are prepared to eliminate their profound influence in the lives of children with learning disabilities.

CHAPTER FOUR

Dr. Mark's Fight Against Injustice

*Why should kids care about themselves when others
act as if they don't care about them?*

"In the little world in which children have their existence whosoever brings them up, there is nothing so finally perceived and so finally felt, as injustice." Charles Dickens (1868) certainly didn't realize when he wrote those words in 1861 that more than a century later they would epitomize the treatment of children and adults with learning disabilities. Today, the injustices that are so "finally felt" are daily experiences that make our children feel inadequate, incapable, unworthy, unattractive, unwanted, unloved, unable—or even worse—unwilling to try. They are perceptions, attitudes, thoughts, and actions that create an environment lacking in respect and warmth. It is an environment where questions go unanswered, offers to help are rejected, discipline is based on failure and punishment, children are excluded from normal and close contact, and basic rights are misused. These are the very experiences that sabotage the Dr. Mark Messages that are critical for children's thinking, feeling, and acting. Since children are a thought away from their destinies, we must remove the obstacles and barrier that deform rather than reform their thinking.

During my tenure as president of the Beaumont Learning Disabilities Association, I had numerous opportunities to hear heartfelt stories from parents, teachers, and children with learning challenges that reflected one injustice after another. I came to realize that injustices never discriminated. These mental viruses, that are all too pervasive among parents, educators, and the public at large, affected children regardless of race, socioeconomic status, ethnic origin or parents' vocations.

Victor was a perfect example of a young child who had suffered more injustice in his short nine years of life than most people did over a lifetime. Even though he was just starting in third grade, Victor had already been branded with a dreadful reputation and was considered a most unpopular student to have in a class. On the second day of third grade, I found him standing out in the hall. His teacher was emphatic, "Victor will not be welcome in my class the rest of the year!" I will never forget his disheartened look; it had only taken this third- grade teacher one day to reject him. There was no question how inadequate, incapable, unworthy, unattractive and unwanted Victor must have felt. It was no surprise that his behaviors had deteriorated from year to year; what behavior should we expect from a student rejected so quickly?

I immediately went to the school principal and asked for Victor to be part of my alternative classroom for five- through nine-year-olds. Concerned about his welfare and with a sigh of what I imagine was relief, she was all too happy to grant my request. I escorted Victor into my room, put my hands on his shoulders, and looked him square in the eyes, "Victor, I want you in my classroom. I don't want you for one day, one week or one month; I want you for the entire year." That day, Victor received something he had seldom encountered in his prior years at school—unconditional acceptance. Sadly, it was an unfamiliar feeling to him. Victor was more accustomed to rejection from adults and his peers.

Harvey could hardly be seen in the kindergarten class that I was observing. Surrounded by a cardboard partition that prevented him from seeing out and his classmates seeing in, he performed his duties in solitude. When I inquired about this treatment, his teacher explained that until Harvey began acting like a five-year-old, he would be excluded from the rest of the class. The other children appeared amused by his separation. Harvey, on the other hand, exhibited a blend of embarrassment at my presence and defiance against his teacher for being banished from the regular environment. Removing him from any contact with his classmates may have been an expedient solution for Harveys' teacher. As in so many other instances when ridicule is employed as discipline, successful re-entry of children once labeled "bad" is hard to accomplish. Peers become much less willing to accept children who have been segregated as a means of enforcement of rules.

Danae was a middle school-aged girl with a severe visual motor deficit. She came home from school one day with a worksheet to help her study for the next day's social studies examination. Danae's parents reviewed what she had written on the worksheet and asked, "What does this say?" Sadly, she had no clue. Because of her disability, Danae could barely take notes from information she heard. Nevertheless, she was expected to study what she had ineffectively copied from the board. Danae's parents set out for the school without delay to discuss this urgent matter with her teacher. They met him as he was about to leave the school parking lot. They inquired, "Mr. Davis, can you tell us what this sheet represents?" Confused, Mr. Davis stated, "I am sorry but the words seem too unintelligible to read. Why do you ask?" Danae's father replied, "This is the sheet my daughter brought home to study for tomorrow's social studies examination." "Impossible!" the teacher barked. "Yes, quite impossible to do anything with this, isn't it?" the parent agreed.

Many parents and children experience the injustices of our system that rob them of the ability to succeed in life. They have every reason to express anger and act out. Martin Luther King, Jr., the eloquent orator, civil rights activist, and Nobel Peace Prize recipient, noted, "The ultimate measure of a man is not where he stands in moments of comfort and convenience, but where he stands at times of challenge and controversy." The expressions of injustices outlined in this chapter are not about airing a laundry list of wrongs in an attempt to make something right. They are about sounding an alarm that has long been silent, calling everyone to take inventory and ask, "Are there injustices within our schools, homes, and community that must be rectified?"

Society cannot afford to be lukewarm over injustices that rob children of their enthusiasm, courage, motivation, and confidence. Society cannot be apathetic over the "internal bruises" that suffocate the flame of hope and excitement necessary for children to burn the midnight oil when other kids are fast asleep. Society must learn to care enough for the fallen to lift them up and remove the sharp sword often found thrust within the heart of struggling learners.

The following seven injustices are presented to help illuminate the suffering of children with learning problems as well as shed light on the actions of adults who work in their behalf. These injustices cannot be eliminated through some mental exercise or by merely reading a book. All parents and educators must realize that it is the responsibility of even the least affected to look out for the welfare of all children, regardless of the needs of their own.

A hear-no-evil, see-no-evil, speak-no-evil position cannot be tolerated if we are to rectify the injustices that invade our communities and rob our children of their futures. The injustices are about truths that often interfere and sabotage children's pursuit of success, large or small. At first glance they may appear to denigrate the work of educators. This is not my intention. I have the strongest affection for the education profession and am an educator myself. However, I will not let my affinity for teaching cloud the needs and concerns of the children. Even as a teacher, my allegiance is first and foremost to children. Always, the welfare of the children should prevail.

Injustice #1

The Hero-Goat Syndrome: We place the high performer on the pedestal and the low performer in the cellar.

Many sports stars have experienced being cheered one minute and booed the next. A touchdown pass or an interception made the difference of whose shoulders they rode after the game, or whose hot seat they filled. The great runner Ben Johnson, who was stripped of the Olympic Gold medal for taking steroids, was a hero one minute and a goat the next. People ride the crest of success one day and fall doomed to the cellar the next.

It is a grave injustice that some school personnel can be so insensitive with our children. Youngsters with learning disabilities often watch as countless others receive the accolades. For instance, my son recently told me about the list of children who made the A and A/B honor roll. "How did you know?" I asked. Painfully, he recounted that the list of names was taped to the wall for everyone to see. That practice may be wonderful for the honor roll students who probably already felt good dozens of times throughout the grading period. Many other children feel like goats since their performances rarely measure up to that level of recognition. Furthermore, some children chide or tease other children whose names are not among the elite, or begin to think of themselves as better because of their academic performance.

I will never forget a little girl named Kristi, who was part of a girl's softball team I coached one summer. Early in the season I told the girls, "You can hit a dozen home runs and I won't hug you any harder than if you strike out a dozen times. The key is in doing your best." On this particular day, Kristi had just struck out at bat. She walked back to the dugout with her eyes watering and chin quivering. I followed her, knelt down in front of her, and said, "Kristi, I don't want you to get a hit." She looked at me with a startled stare. I continued, "Before you ever get a hit, I want you to learn how to take three strikes without getting so down on yourself." This was my attempt to give her permission to do poorly without taking it so hard. It was also an attempt to help her see a more important goal while at bat: to take a chance at the plate without the worry of defeat. It was not surprising to find every player cheering one another that day, despite their mistakes.

School administrators, teachers, and yes, parents must become cognizant of activities that perpetuate the Hero-Goat Syndrome. Competitive activities such as spelling bees qualify if a teacher does not establish an environment of acceptance for all children, regardless of their differences in performance. Overt attention and praise given only to the best readers will cause slower readers to withdraw. The more attention that is paid to the best artwork, the fewer paintings by others less talented can be expected. The magnification of one child's strength can result in the magnification of another child's weakness.

Teachers of young children experience this regularly. If youngsters overhear the teacher praising a child for some great work, other young learners immediately converge on the teacher demanding equal time. "Teacher, teacher, look at my picture!" cry the classmates. What they really mean is, "Teacher, teacher, tell me my work is just as good." The children who already see their work as inferior often say nothing. They quietly stop exercising that skill, believing they will never "measure up" in their teacher's eyes. The result? The skill goes undeveloped, their performance lags and they live up to the unspoken expectation that they can't achieve. Is this how we want to guide our children?

One other example is worth mentioning. I attended a band concert one year at my daughter's school. Before Charlotte played with the eighth-grade band, we listened to the seventh graders perform. Their piece was beautiful. At its conclusion, the bandleader explained why the students had played so well. He asked the A and B honor roll students in the band to stand; practically all the children jumped to their feet. Their academic proficiency was his explanation for the beautiful music, silently conveying that students making grades below an A or a B could not possibly perform at such a level of excellence. Not only did parents hear his remarks, many children heard them as well. My son, who is not used to making high grades, had a new seed planted in his mind that night, one that was untrue and unnecessary to hear. After the recital he told me that he could never be part of the band. When I asked him why, he replied, "Because I'm not a good enough student."

There is nothing wrong with pointing out our children's strengths. This injustice prevails, when adults over-inflate some students' performances at the exclusion of others. Our children would be better served by celebrating the achievements, however large or small, of all students.

INJUSTICE #2
Mailclerkitis: We label, sort, and categorize children.

A skill necessary for success among mail clerks involves labeling, sorting, and categorizing mail. Mail is labeled for different cities, sorted for a variety of weights, and categorized by priority. The public depends on the mastery of those skills and becomes annoyed when mistakes occur.

School systems, families, and society in general are also in the labeling, sorting, and categorizing business. In this case the packages we label, sort, and categorize are far more precious than the most highly insured mail—they are our children. Children all over the country are being separated through the misuse of standardized examinations. Tests are being used to tell children what they can't do more than they are being used as an indication of their chances for success. Too many children with learning disabilities are labeled and sorted into classrooms based more on the label than on the individual needs of the student. Predictions about ability, award ceremonies, school tracking, and other means of segregation all play a part in this massive business of categorizing children.

This labeling and sorting is not an exact science. While the initial diagnosis can be important as a guideline to steer educators towards appropriate methods and services, the improper use of such findings can be detrimental to the education of children. Kristin Gist, my sister and director of the San Diego Children's Hospital Diagnostic Clinic, spoke to educators about children affected by substance abuse. She insisted, "Children affected by substance abuse cannot all be treated the same, as if they all manifest the same symptoms. The necessary treatment plan for one child may be entirely different from the treatment of other children." The same is true for children with learning problems. The treatment for one may differ greatly from the treatment of others.

The minds of children play a key role in their differences and complicate the delicate art of understanding children. They are also affected by their hearts, souls, and spirits. Show me children whose hearts, souls, and spirits are behind impossible dreams and I will show you miracles.

Children with learning problems do not fit neatly into standard-sized white envelopes that require the standard 37-cent stamp. We must take children out of these tightly sealed envelopes and stop licking, stamping, and sending them on their way as if they are ready to be mailed and delivered without proper postage. Proper postage in our schools is a broader understanding and acceptance of all children's capabilities. What will the postage cost? An increase in the desire to do what we know is right, not what saves the most money.

A continuum of characteristics distinguishes one child with learning disabilities from another. Until we learn to recognize and celebrate these differences, our children will continue to receive the message that says they are worth only enough attention to categorize, prepackage, and deliver them to a classroom. Elimination of this injustice will mean greater integration among all peers, greater acceptance among family members, and greater appreciation by the teaching team.

INJUSTICE #3
A One-Size-Fits-All Mentality: We don't always teach the way some students learn.

All children deserve equal opportunity to succeed; few would argue this point. Many believe equal opportunity can only be provided through a one-size-fits-all structure and vehemently resist differential treatment that is driven by the different ways that children learn. One of the most common responses to recommendations that children with learning problems receive differential treatment is, "You can't do that for one child without doing it for all children."

We don't always teach the way children learn. Even worse, some teachers perform without considering the needs of the learner. Many schools frequently magnify and exacerbate our children's disabilities by using inappropriate teaching methods. In other words, the focus is on teaching without consideration for the impact on student learning. In this case, where does the disability really lie? Does it lie within the learner or the teacher? I believe the latter.

There are times while teaching at the university when I reprimand my teacher education candidates with the exclamation, "Stop interfering with my teaching by raising your hands to ask questions. It is distracting to my teaching when your hands are raised. I am more concerned about my teaching than your confusion. Please, just let me teach!"

This exchange results in all sorts of disgusted looks, confusion, and antagonism among the teacher education candidates. Before one candidate had caught on to the point I was trying to get them to understand, she challenged, "How in the world can you teach if you are unwilling to answer our questions?" I retorted, "Now, do you see the absurdity of ignoring the learner in the teaching process?" In classrooms across the nation, teachers must make sure that their method of teaching matches the way children learn. That includes children with learning disorders. We don't expect a physician to treat a patient with the wrong medicine, or a lawyer to go to court with the wrong briefs. Accordingly, we must not expect teachers to use lesson plans appropriate for one child to teach another.

Mel Levine (2002), a prominent learning expert, who wrote the book, *A Mind at a Time,* concluded that a teacher who acquires background knowledge about children's learning can understand the way in which students have their personal ways of learning. From this, Levine says, "Teachers can generate ideas about how to teach" (p. 308).

Rather than treating children as if they have a one-size-fits-all learning system, Dr. Levine (2002) outlined eight neurodevelopmental systems that reflect different learning patterns among children. The eight neurodevelopmental systems include attention control, memory, language, spatial ordering, sequential ordering, motor, higher thinking, and social thinking. Teachers educated in Levine's neurodevelopmental systems are more apt to increase instructional efficiency and effectiveness. This form of teaching is also more likely to inspire children to work on their weaknesses while building on their strengths. Finally, this way of teaching will encourage adults to monitor all aspects of children's development.

The homogenization of the classroom is unrealistic as long as we know that children learn differently and at different rates. The time allegedly saved through this style of teaching is precious time wasted on our children. We must accept as fact that everyone has a specific learning style or unique neurodevelopmental system, just as everyone's fingerprints are unique. Compatibility between a student's learning characteristics and the teacher's instructional method is a key for promoting success. In the end, the burden for modification falls on the educator, not the child, although our past history would suggest otherwise.

One mother told me about a conversation she had with her daughter's teacher. The mother suggested, "Mrs. Brown, you might alleviate Katrina's crying when she makes mistakes by using a stuffed teddy bear, describing it as someone who needs to learn strategies for making mistakes gracefully. Let's tell

Katrina a story about the stuffed teddy bear's crying episodes and our need to find a child who can teach the teddy bear more positive responses to mistakes." This type of mentoring technique can be very effective for young children who personify inanimate objects, seeing objects such as stuffed teddy bears as lifelike creatures. Mrs. Brown insisted, "There is no way Katrina can be allowed to mentor a teddy bear without all the other children demanding the same treatment." Mrs. Brown's disturbing insistence is not unusual among people who believe that equal opportunity comes through the same treatment.

I was able to illuminate this injustice to Katrina's teacher through a poignant story about a child who began to choke on some food in the cafeteria. The child lay on the floor. As the teacher fell to her knees she saw the fright in the child's eyes. At the moment the child felt a sense of relief that help was at hand, the teacher replied, "I am so sorry. I cannot in good conscience dislodge the obstacle in your throat for fear of upsetting your classmates. It would not be fair to help one without helping the others." The light bulb in Mrs. Brown's mind went off. "Oh, I see. The only way to provide children with equal opportunity is through providing them differential treatment."

The reluctance to differentiate learning and behavior plans is an injustice that must come to an abrupt halt. There can never be a level playing field as long as people see as, unfair practice modifications and accommodations designed to facilitate learning. Children may lack the skills to effectively and efficiently transfer information from the board. Children may demonstrate a processing problem that slows their response when asked a question. Children may exhibit aberrant behaviors due to a lack of social competence. In each case, fairness is accessed when—and only when—children's differences are respected, appreciated, and celebrated through differential and appropriate individualized treatment. One of the most powerful and influential videos marketed today is Richard Lavoie's *How Difficult Can This Be.* Lavoie (1989) concludes with a discussion about fairness. He expresses strong contempt for those who refuse to differentiate. Lavoie challenges the viewers to look at the world through the eyes of children with learning disabilities. In doing so, viewers are much more inclined to empathize rather than codify children. It is through this awakening that a one-size-fits-all mentality gives way to justice and fairness for all.

INJUSTICE #4

The Pyramid Mentality: We recognize a few at the expense of many.

My wife and I recently attended a two-hour award ceremony at my daughter's school. It went something like this: "Ladies and gentlemen, students and faculty, the winner of the science award this year is Margaret White. The winner of the award for outstanding achievement in math is Margaret White. This year's award in English is presented to Margaret White." Approximately 300 children sat through that two-hour ceremony, where Margaret White and a cadre of perhaps five other students captured 99 percent of the awards. As the event progressed, I watched the faces of many of the children change from excitement to despair, to boredom or embarrassment. I imagined them murmuring, "Why am I here? Are you trying to motivate me through humiliation? Who is this ceremony for? Certainly not the majority of us!"

Many children with learning problems long for recognition, especially in the one area where they work the hardest—academic performance. However, most school-based award ceremonies are designed to recognize only the top athletes and the highest academic performers. As a society, are we comfortable ignoring the salient contributions that the "rest of the world" provides in favor of attention only to this highly selective group? We must challenge the athletic and intellectual beauty pageants found in many schools. This does not necessarily mean a ban of such pageants. It does, however, challenge educators to develop more creative ways to recognize all students who demonstrate attributes worthy of recognition.

We have taught children there is no master race, superior ethnic origin, or preferred gender. Yet we continually act as though there is a master intellect. This must stop. The primary responsibility of the school environment is to develop a sense of capability among all children. The selective recognition we give to only the crème de la crème among our students, through various contests and ceremonies, is not always the best vehicle to reinforce this idea. Grandmother used to say, "If you can't say anything good, don't say anything." Unfortunately, the fact that nothing is said speaks volumes.

Children who are most proficient have a greater opportunity to become more proficient. Many children with learning problems, who have the most deficiencies, habitually receive the least practice to remedy or compensate for those deficiencies. By selectively acknowledging the achievements of so few, we create a breeding ground for the rest of our children to take an "I don't care" attitude. Why should kids care about themselves when others act as if they don't care for them? This malnourishment of our children's self-esteem and self-concepts should be grounds for educational malpractice.

INJUSTICE #5

Academic Overexposure: We minimize the importance of life-abilities or self-success habits.

Some time ago I asked Dr. Lucious Waites, who directed a program at the Scottish Rites Hospital for young people like me with dyslexia, "How did I excel academically despite my childhood struggles in school?" Dr. Waites sat back in his chair and quickly responded, "Tenacity, perseverance, determination, and willpower." I've often wondered how many thousands of children fail because of a lack of what I call 'life-abilities' or 'self-success' habits. Many struggling learners have enough intellect to succeed; but in the "real world" intellect is often not enough.

In his most insightful book, *The Misunderstood Child*, Larry Silver referred to learning disabilities as life disabilities. Silver (1998) claimed that disabilities interfere with every aspect of children's and adolescents' lives—at home, with friends, in sports, in activities. This being true, it becomes critical for parents and educators to develop life-abilities as an antidote to the life disabilities that often paralyze progress and leave despair in their wakes.

Life-abilities or self-success habits include confidence, motivation, persistence, perseverance, determination, tolerance, risk-taking, caring, graceful mistake making, resisting temptation, delaying gratification, resilience, and problem solving. These abilities or skills are the backbone, the bricks and mortar that build a solid foundation for academic learning. Yet we often spend more time making our children study for a science test than shaping their desire to study. Why do we commit such educational transgression? Schools are so busy teaching reading, writing, and arithmetic that too little attention is given to teaching tenacity, determination, perseverance, and willpower. Children with learning challenges must receive help to feel confident, no matter their academic performance.

Few children experience success every day. Subsequently, we must give life-abilities or self-success skills more importance than we currently do. Will we be taking quality time away from instruction by doing so? Will we be decreasing time for children to learn to read, write, and do arithmetic? No! In the end, children will benefit from more instructional time, not less. Children who feel better about themselves and others, and who have a sense of respect for their work, will spend less time engaging in behaviors that interfere with learning. Children who persevere will concentrate longer on a difficult assignment. Children willing to take risks will pursue more learning opportunities.

One teacher, Mr. Borum, was a perfect example of the tug-of-war between focusing on academics and incorporating success strategies as part of the instruction in our schools. Mr. Borum was three years into the profession when I met him. As our conversation began, he appeared a bit uneasy at what he was about to say. Did he think that because I was a contract therapist working for the school district, I was looking for a reason to jerk his probationary period out from under his feet? Or was it something else?

I waited patiently for the gate to swing open. When it did Mr. Borum spoke with the passion of an enraged bull. "Dr. Cooper, there's something wrong with my teaching!" I remained quiet; I could see that Mr. Borum was in no mood to be rescued. He continued, "I spend practically all my time forcing reading, writing, and arithmetic into the minds of my students when I know good and well there are other equally important lessons. I act as if these kids are robots, programmed to care only about what I teach. They're children! They're kids who want to play, talk, laugh, run, argue, fight, tease, tattle, and throw temper tantrums. Do I act as if I care about who they are? No! I'm so busy forcing them to learn academics that I'm not even beginning to reach their hearts and souls. In the long run, my students will learn the subjects; that's for sure. But they may never learn some of the things that are so much more important, like diligence, orderliness, boldness, caring, responsibility, productivity, delayed gratification, risk-taking."

While he refueled his lungs, I replied, "Mr. Borum, what stops you from teaching those other thoughts and ideas along with reading, writing, and arithmetic?" He fell silent for quite some time, as if he was rehearsing something that he had considered saying more than once. "I teach the way the school tells me to teach, according to their mission," he softly commented. "The school's mission?" I echoed. At that moment, the door flew open and his class returned from recess. Mr. Borum raised his head, his eyes full of sorrow and despair, and emphatically repeated, "That's right; the school's mission."

I give us an F for failing to teach the very skills that can make our children successful with whatever academic training they receive. Yes, I want children to learn how to read, write, and add, subtract, multiply, and divide. What better climate for learning these skills than one where children are also given a solid foundation for learning, one that includes the will to achieve, the desire to persist toward achievement, and the success skills to express such achievement?

A private school in Houston, Texas provided a wonderful example of how academics and success skills can work together. A few years ago, I was invited to present the commencement address to approximately thirteen graduating seniors, all of whom had learning disabilities of some kind. When I had the opportunity to meet each of these students, I was struck by their remarkable social acuity. They knew exactly how to introduce themselves, from proper body posture to appropriate eye contact. Each senior communicated perfectly without adult supervision. Their verbal expressions were exact and proper. It was evident these young people had been taught two things—academics and social success skills. The teaching, monitoring, and reinforcement occurred as the students simultaneously learned reading, writing, and arithmetic. There was no question that these seniors had been fortified with important success skills that would enable them to maximize their academic training.

Children with learning problems face difficult assignments on a daily basis.

It takes courage to tackle such assignments. Children with learning problems need to devote more time to homework and have less time for leisure. It takes self-discipline to engage in such devotion. Children with learning problems need to do today what they may want to put off for tomorrow. Such a work ethic requires delayed gratification. If children with learning problems do not acquire habits of thinking such as a commitment to learning, determination, tenacity, risk-taking, problem solving, and a willingness to face defeat, then no amount of knowledge building or skill enhancement will help. Without the various habits of thinking that affect work ethic and productivity, all other matters lose their meaning.

Norman Vincent Peale, a minister, author, philosopher, and orator, claimed, "Any fact facing us is not as important as our attitude toward it, for that determines our success or failure" (cited in Anderson & McKee 1990). Parents and teachers helping children with learning problems must face this fact. These children need to engage in habitual thinking that propels them to decode yet another word easily read by others, to stand erect when required to compete in a spelling bee, and to write one more paragraph when the midnight oil has already burnt out. The former Green Bay Packer coach Vince Lombardi echoed such a sentiment when he emphatically stated, "The difference between a successful person and others is not a lack of strength, not a lack of knowledge, but rather a lack of will" (cited in Anderson & McKee).

Schools and families must demand that teaching of success habits become an integral part of education. As children acquire these habits, we must celebrate them, regardless of their academic performance. We must design opportunities for children to study and practice these success habits, which will, in turn, increase their level of academic performance. There must be a whole-school effort, involving family and community support, to create an environment based on character, where behaviors such as caring, courage, respect, honesty, hard work, and self-control are modeled, labeled, demonstrated, rehearsed, monitored, and celebrated.

Winston Churchill, author, orator, prime minister, and Nobel Prize for literature recipient, had a stuttering problem, yet he spoke and spoke successfully. An editor told Louisa May Alcott, a successful author, that she would never write anything that had popular appeal. Yet, she wrote and wrote successfully. A music teacher told Enrico Caruso, one of the world's great opera stars, that he had no voice. Yet, he sang and sang successfully. The true genius behind these giants in politics, literature, and music was success habits that involved determination, tenacity, and a strong work ethic. Children with learning problems must be taught habits that will assist them in taking small steps toward success, steps that one day may leave giant footprints. Success Strategy #11 in Chapter Five outlines seven habits designed to transform those small steps into giant footprints.

INJUSTICE #6

Inferiority Mentality: We treat children as though they are dumb, inferior, and incapable.

On the six o'clock T.V. news one evening, one of the commentators was recognizing the quality of work performed by a child, Michael, who had a learning problem. He exhorted, "We need to give credit to Michael, and the countless other unsung heroes whose efforts are Herculean despite their struggles." "Bravo," I thought, "he really understands the nature of learning challenges." But elation quickly changed to anger as the commentator concluded, "Because Michael is so bright, he could not be helped through special education." I could just imagine the shoulders that slumped when children in special education heard such a disclaimer.

Many years in the teaching profession have taught me, first-hand, two things about the Inferiority Mentality injustice. First, there are thousands of people who believe that children with learning disabilities are dumb, inferior, and incapable. This idea persists among parents, siblings, classmates, community patrons, and teachers. In this instance, it existed with the newscaster who shared the message with tens of thousands of viewers, some of whom were children with a history of special education. Second, too little is being done to destroy this gross misconception, one that sabotages our children's positive thinking.

A female student in my class was making a good point yesterday about the important match between teaching method and children's learning styles. "Dr. Cooper, I can see your reasoning behind the match between teaching method and children's learning styles. Teachers must make sure that they teach the way children learn. This may be especially true for children with learning problems." "Yes! Yes! Yes!" I reflected with great enthusiasm and personal satisfaction. I was proud to witness that my students were, indeed, listening to me. Unfortunately, the rest of her story was a sharp pin that quickly deflated my ego. She added, "My child doesn't have a learning disability because he is too smart. The trouble he's having in school is because of the improper match of teaching and learning styles." My heart sank at hearing another person whose definition of learning disability rejects the possibility that someone can be smart and still challenged.

An educational campaign is necessary throughout our schools, neighborhoods, and communities to help people understand that children with learning disabilities are very capable. Mel Levine (2002), suggested in his book, *A Mind at a Time,* that students, teachers, and parents need to better understand the many facets of the mind discussed under Injustice Three about the one-size-fits-all mentality. According to Levine, parents and teachers must focus on the progress of the eight systems. In doing so, the parents and teachers will be more inclined to prepare the learning environment for the children rather than requiring the children to be prepared for the learning environment.

Children, parents, and teachers should participate in activities designed to increase understanding of the different neurodevelopmental systems described by Levine (2002). Children need to see the banners and hear the announcements that learning problems have more to do with differences than deficits. A deficit model is unnecessary. Children with learning problems need not see themselves as patients sick with some irreparable disease. They must see their abilities, their potential, as well as their uniqueness. Of course, this can best happen when parents and teachers apply similar understanding and embrace Levine's (2002) assertion that the environment most conducive for learning will be the environment that reflects all kinds of minds.

A number of years ago, 300 adolescents attended a motivational session I offered to help them cope more successfully in their classrooms despite their struggles. During the forty-five-minute presentation most of them seemed attentive. However, very few were daring enough to visit with me after the presentation. One boy did write a letter a week later.

"I liked your speech, it was a good one. My mom and I liked it. You are good with learning difficulties. I am improving in my reading class! It is hard to work with it. I am glad to meet someone that has learning difficulties. I am best at sports than school. I am just like you."

Love John

The speech was an important moment for John. His misconception about being inferior himself began to crack. A mind alignment emerged. John heard my presentation as the testimonial of a person with learning challenges who had succeeded in life and he began to think of himself as someone who could perform as well. So often we ask children to identify with intellectual giants such as Thomas Edison and Albert Einstein, or athletes like Bruce Jenner, or movie stars like Tom Cruise or Cher. Most children have trouble identifying with such famous people. As an alternative, introduce them to local people, whom they can see, hear and touch. Ask your favorite newspaper reporter to write an article about area residents who have succeeded despite daily academic struggles. There are more successful people than you might think living your community who grew up with learning disabilities.

John is one voice among many. Children and teens like him need support that goes beyond their immediate family and teachers. They need support within their peer group. Until this support becomes more pervasive, many children with learning disabilities will remain hidden under the guise of inferiority. As a result, we all will miss their efforts and their contributions.

The peer group is one of the most powerful influences on children's developing views of themselves, their self-importance, self-appreciation, and self-affirmation. Children spend an endless amount of time obsessing about the views of others. Particularly, during the middle and high school years, the opinions of others carve deep tracks in the minds and hearts of students. Nowhere is this more acutely felt than from their own peers. Be it subtle looks, or outright comments, peers can bolster an ego or tear it apart in a matter of seconds.

Struggling learners have many opportunities to feel the fangs of injustice among their peer group. Lowell was one such child. He made no bones about how he felt, "I'm tired of people calling me gay blade, queerdoe, and fairy." Lowell was a young guy who, despite his efforts achieved little success in school. His learning disabilities were accentuated by a real lack of social competence. His peers complained that he did not know when to shut up and when to leave them alone.

When I met Lowell, there were no strategies in place to facilitate understanding or change in Lowell's peer group. He was in an inclusive program, but one doomed to failure because of the lack of attention to peer education and acceptance. While Lowell was given lessons about social skills, his peers received no instruction—as if their socialization skills were already polished. The fact was, they weren't. I often noticed Lowell sitting against the wall, having little contact with the rest of his class. The experiences necessary to successfully integrate Lowell and his peer group were being ignored.

Lowell's teacher was already at her wit's end. She felt paralyzed by the breadth and depth of the problem. "How in the world can I teach these academic subjects as well as teach Lowell and everyone else to like each other?" The magnifying glass she held over the problem seemed glued to her nose. She was underestimating two things—the ability of the children to change their minds about Lowell and her ability to facilitate such change. Rather than try to explain it, I chose to demonstrate. That afternoon I told the class a story about a little boy named Jeffrey who was alienated, separated, and isolated from his group. The children's hearts sank when they heard that Jeffrey had never attended a birthday party until third grade. Feelings of empathy rose in the kids as I told them that Jeffrey's classmates treated him as an outcast because he struggled in school and looked odd as a result of months of chemotherapy and radiation treatment. There was absolute silence when the children learned that Jeffrey never enjoyed another birthday party because he died two months after that first one.

I let the children sit in silence, giving them time to absorb their feelings. Soon heated discussion followed. I listened while children attacked the insensitivity and lack of compassion among Jeffrey's peer group. I knew they were hooked. Very quickly and easily, I began steering their thoughts away from the story of Jeffrey to the reality of their own classroom by asking, "Are there people in your school or classroom who are treated like Jeffrey?" "I am," Lowell responded very softly. The weight of his confession hung heavy in the air. Fortunately, one of the classmates who carried significant influence with the peer group shared, "Lowell is right. He is treated like Jeffrey."

This was an important step and a beginning. At that precise moment, the children, perhaps for the first time, saw Lowell in a different light—not as a weird, dumb kid but as a person. His teacher knew that within her grasp were discussions that could change the thinking among Lowell's classmates.

Lowell's story had a happy ending. He no longer had to hide under the mask of inferiority. No longer were his efforts and contributions ignored. While Lowell and his classmates did not all become best friends, they did begin to show more friendliness and compassion toward one another. Lowell's teacher learned that the minds of children are much more open once the heart is engaged.

INJUSTICE #7
Apathetic Mentality: We perpetuate injustice through inaction.

Imagine the millions of bystanders who watched while staggering numbers of Jews were murdered in the Holocaust. Imagine the bystanders who watched while thousands of African-Americans were treated as slaves. Who were these bystanders? The "bystanders" are the many people who pretend to see no evil and hear no evil and, of course, speak of no evil. Bystanders are those of us who are willing to let injustice occur without lifting a finger or saying a word. Bystanders exert a powerful influence: They can move others toward empathy or indifference.

Parents and educators doing nothing but standing by and watching injustice occur commit the greatest of all injustices. In the process, bias, misconception and misunderstanding reign. We allow the misconceptions regarding children with learning disabilities to go unchallenged. These children are thought of as dumb by their peers, inferior by some parents, and incapable by certain teachers. We facilitate the use of teaching methods that are not compatible with our children's learning mode. We consent to the practice of labeling, sorting, and categorizing our children through the misuse of testing. Our silence tacitly condones the practice of reinforcing the efforts of children who typically make the best grades while ignoring many of our children who struggle to stay afloat, but who work just as hard. Our lack of protest encourages schools to emphasize the basic subjects without teaching important self-success skills such as confidence, tolerance, motivation, risk-taking, and perseverance. Finally, our apathy allows wrongdoing to not only live . . . but to destroy our children, their lives and their futures.

Some of us are losing our ability to *feel* the facts about the plights of struggling learners. Information without feeling is not knowledge and can lead only to public irresponsibility and indifference and conceivably ruin. Many of the problems involving children with learning disabilities lie not with our leaders but with us. It is no longer enough to know the facts about the injustices. We must *feel* the facts that we know. We must never forget that the vital factor that separates mediocrity from greatness, success from failure, and winning from losing, is feeling. We must open our eyes, uncover our ears and speak out with a clear and urgent message. It is not until we act on the emotions provoked by these injustices that we can expect our footsteps to be followed.

Children are the hope for tomorrow. Those who raise and teach them are the hope for today. They must see themselves as role models capable and willing to cause injustice to perish and crumble. They must see themselves as role models capable and willing to brighten the lives of children through just principles that will last a lifetime.

A preacher in India once said, "It is better to shun the bait than struggle in the snare." Many children with learning problems have been snared by the injustices discussed here. They have been snared by a tendency to place them on the sideline, by an omission from recognition, by a tunnel vision that maximizes reading, writing, and arithmetic while minimizing the three Ps—persistence, patience, and perseverance—by a practice that insists all children learn the same way at the same rate, by a perception that learning problems and intelligence are mutually exclusive, and finally by an unwillingness of many bystanders to say, "Enough is enough!"

Our children who struggle can ill afford apathy toward such examples of "wrongthinking". We need fewer people afraid to join the fray. In recommending a strategy for change, 1952 Nobel Peace Prize winner, Albert Schweitzer (1963) admonished us to increasingly appreciate those who perform small and obscure deeds on behalf of others. Schweitzer suggested that the impact of those who perform small and obscure deeds is a thousand times stronger than the acts of those who receive wide public recognition for their performances. Badaracco (2002), the author of *Leading Quietly*, agreed. He recommended that we not limit our definition of great leaders to those who transform major companies, reshape society, or risk lives. According to Badaracco (2002), "The great leaders needed are people who move patiently, carefully, and incrementally. They do what is right—their organizations, for the people around them, and for themselves—inconspicuously and without casualties " (1). Our struggling learners will also depend on not only those who carry the torch, but also those who encourage the torchbearers. Once the voices of a nation speak, there will be more compelling reasons for change and more optimistic reasons to expect those changes.

While eradication of the injustices is necessary, Dr. Mark's Strategies, discussed in the next chapter, can help prevent injustices from gaining ground. The strategies help create within the home, school, and community a more positive environment, free from threats to our children. The very fabric of our country is based on liberty and justice for all. "For all" includes children with learning problems. This liberty and justice cannot be gained without a willingness to employ strategies designed to affect the very hearts and minds of children.

CHAPTER FIVE

DR. MARK'S SUCCESS STRATEGIES

Show children where they are going rather than limiting the vision to where they are.

"I accept my child just the way he is!" I cannot tell you how often I hear such exclamations while parents hyperventilate at the same time.

I know how much Mom and Dad wanted to accept me "just the way I was." I also know how much they feared for my academic welfare during the first half of my life. I know as a parent who has raised a child with learning challenges the difficulty in accepting anything outside the norm, especially if the differences cause worry. It is no wonder parents hyperventilate when faced with raising struggling learners. Society is more accepting of the norm. Parents feel more capable of raising children who fit the norm. Teachers have fewer challenges when faced with "normal" children.

Parents, in an effort to hide their frustration, disappointment, and despair, immerse themselves in activities designed to correct the problems in hopes that their children will become more normalized. Their lives consist of finding tutors, enrolling children in summer schools, soliciting special treatment, spending countless hours helping with assignments, insisting on extra credit for school work, or inquiring about incomplete assignments. While sometimes heroic and regularly worthy of praise, all these efforts prevent them from experiencing the sweet and tender taste of true acceptance of their children—learning challenges and all. The quest to let go and fully accept children just the way they are is easier said than done. It does not happen overnight, nor is there a twelve-step program that guarantees success. It is mainly done through trial and error, precariously balancing action with non-action, pressure with patience. This is not a criticism; this is reality.

I was a child whose parents, especially Mom, reached beyond their grasp to do anything to maximize learning opportunities for me and increase my probability of acceptance, affirmation, and achievement. I am also the parent of a child with learning challenges whose needs require extra effort. All too often my wife and I walk a fine line, trying to decipher whether we are applying too much or too little pressure. The line between accepting children just the way they are and the desire to heighten achievement expectations is very thin. We never truly know the proper balance. This reality makes it very difficult for us, as it is for other parents of children with learning disorders, to do the right thing at the right time.

Teachers are not spared from this reality either. They are also trying to discriminate among mixed messages sent by administrators, other educators, learned professionals, and the students themselves. Teachers long to accept children just the way they are. By way of their profession, however, they are also empowered to make them "other" than they are. What makes it difficult is that two contradictory messages are never far away: "I like you just the way you are," and "I don't like you enough to leave you that way."

The hopes, dreams, and expectations of parents and teachers of children with learning problems are no different than those of other parents and teachers. Where the differences lie are perhaps best illustrated by how we approach questions such as, "What can the child accomplish?" and "What will success look like for this child?" These questions reflect an attempt to make predictions about children's future. Adults in the lives of children with learning problems often stare helplessly at these challenging questions. The adults require an understanding of the minds, hearts, and souls of children, and too few people know enough about these areas to answer such questions with confidence. In the face of such challenges, parents and teachers often adopt a more amenable declaration: "Johnnie, do your best." The emphasis on children doing their very best becomes a more palatable approach, one that appears benign and accepting. Yet, it is also one that is surrounded by landmines and sinkholes.

How do we accomplish these lofty goals of unconditional acceptance and knowing when, and how much, to encourage our children? The answer is not an easy one, and the search for solutions is never ending. I keep a statement taken from a quote by Helen Keller that suggests that I am only one and while I cannot do everything I will not refuse to do the something I can do.

The ten success strategies outlined in this chapter represent the "something" that you and I can do. These strategies encourage parents and teachers of struggling learners to care more than others think is wise, risk more than others think is safe, dream more than others think is practical, and expect more than others think is possible. These strategies also encourage parents and teachers to see normal as an acceptable aberration and realize that the uniqueness of our children lies in their differences, not in their normalcy. In turn, the children will be taught to take pride in their efforts, to understand that self-acceptance and self-affirmation do not have to wait for some elusive accomplishment, *and* to reach their maximum potential.

As we walk out upon the tightrope that is often our daily experience with children with learning disabilities, we do have a safety net. It is our faith that good intentions win out, best efforts will be good enough, and yes, God is merciful.

SUCCESS STRATEGY #1

Acceptance + Expectation = The Pursuit of Happiness and Achievement

This first strategy is the most important, as it lays the groundwork for integrating all the rest of the strategies. Goethe, an internationally acclaimed writer said, "When we treat a man as he is, we make him worse than he is. When we treat him as if he already were what he potentially could be, we make him what he should be." Stop and reread that quote, for it is a two-edged sword ready to strike either a positive or negative chord.

Goethe forewarns, "When we treat a man as he is, we make him worse than he is." No parent or teacher wants to make our struggling learners worse. Their struggles are great enough. Goethe also encourages, "When we treat a man as if he already were what he potentially could be, we make him what he should be!" This statement is also fraught with alarm although it sounds very inviting. Of course, parents and teachers want to anticipate the best and treat their children as having great potential. Such optimistic and positive thinking set a wonderful example for all parties involved in children's education and welfare. It may also be just the bait that entices parents and teachers to set unreasonable performance goals and communicate a lack of acceptance for the children's present performances.

Damned if we do! Damned if we don't! How do parents and teachers accept children just the way they are and simultaneously expect them to reach beyond their present level of performance? There is no more difficult tightrope to walk or peak to climb. Mom swayed from side to side trying to convey acceptance while investing many hours to help me perform better in school. It was hard for me to sense her acceptance as she tried so hard to change me academically. Even though I grew up with this experience, I found myself struggling to find that right balance between unconditional acceptance and prodding my son, Jim, to try harder, work harder, and perform better. The tug-of-war between the two ideas always seemed to create more tension than peace.

Pastor Clif, a preacher in a local church, gave a sermon entitled, "On the Way to a New World." I was enthralled by his comment about the Be-Attitudes, where God gives us a glimpse of where we are going while we spend much of our time fixed on where we are. His reflections were right on target. God knows of the frequent feelings of despair, resignation, and hopelessness among struggling learners and those who raise and teach those learners. Fortunately, He is unwilling to leave us with those feelings without showing us the light and life of His kingdom. This becomes our job as well. Parents and teachers must not hesitate to give children with learning problems a wonderful glimpse of a future filled with hope, optimism, and encouragement. In so doing, they show the children where they are going rather than limiting their vision to where they are.

How do parents and teachers find that happy medium of combining the acceptance of where children are and showing them a glimpse of where they are going? Stephen Covey (1989), an internationally respected leadership authority and author of books such as *The 7 Habits of Highly Effective People,* uses a metaphor he calls "the emotional bank account" to help people gauge how they make deposits or withdrawals into emotional bank accounts. Expressions of kindness, consideration, helpfulness, or patience are examples of emotional deposits. Conversely, expressions of criticism, comparison, put-down, and ridicule are examples of emotional withdrawals.

Covey's metaphor applies equally to expressions conveying acceptance of where children are and heightened expectations for where they are going. In the case of children with learning challenges, an emotional withdrawal reflects parents' and teachers' dissatisfaction with children's performance regardless of effort. The children may demonstrate their very best and yet receive little encouragement. This "dog-eat-dog" mentality withdraws hope, certainty, security, confidence, and self-acceptance from children's emotional bank accounts. The focus is on what the children have not accomplished. The focus is also on what the children "must" accomplish before they receive any display of teacher/parent satisfaction or acceptance. There is no balance between acceptance and expectation and thus no propensity toward happiness or achievement.

An emotional deposit, on the other hand, reflects parents' and teachers' satisfaction with the children without regard to how they presently perform. It reflects the unconditional acceptance that says, "I like you and nothing you do or do not do will deter me from such affection." Pastor Clif did not suggest that God fails to accept our present state while giving us that glimpse of our future state. Quite the contrary; God does both. He revels in and embraces both states. This "unconditional" kind of affection is not earned. It occurs at birth regardless of how much or how loud the newborn screams, "Get me back to where I came from!" This relationship is not permissive. There are boundaries, expectations, rules, and regulations. Nevertheless, the parents and teachers make every effort to appreciate and accept the children whether they stay inside or outside the boundaries.

There is no greater challenge than accepting children as they are. Children who misbehave at home or school often bring out the worst in parents and teachers. Those children make adults feel inadequate and inept. Regardless, parents and teachers must find every ounce of inner strength to resist making the emotional withdrawals and communicate instead the emotional deposits. Even knowing that, I have found myself on many occasions responding to Jim with a barrage of verbal challenges.

"Jim, how are you going to make better grades if you continue to leave your homework assignments at school?"

"Jim, you just aren't trying hard enough."

"Jim, the television is no more than an idiot box that promotes idiocy. It will not complete your homework assignments. Stop taking the easy way out."

"Jim, you aren't giving it your best effort."

Jim once exclaimed, "Dad, you sound like a pinched nerve!" He was right. My statements, like pinched nerves, reflected only his failures to perform and reinforced the idea, "I am what I am and that's all you can stand." Jim's emotional bank account would run in the red upon receiving such messages. How else could he possibly see himself in light of such emotional withdrawals? My statements provided little encouragement for him to dream big and believe that his dreams were not only possible to fulfill, but inevitable. I was neither accepting where Jim was at that time nor giving him a glimpse of where he was going.

Teachers confront the same demons. It is difficult for teachers to look past where children are and project where they are going. Too often the perception of where children are is treated as the prognosis for where they are going. This runs counter to Pastor Clif's exhortation. Ability reflects children's capacities while achievement reflects their present levels of performance. The lack of discrimination between the two confounds the problem and creates the propensity to treat an achievement level as if it equates to a child's maximum capacity. The emphasis of our educational system on individual achievement, via tests, contests, and report cards, further perpetuates this tendency. The result? Teachers inaccurately come to believe, "The children can accomplish no more than they presently demonstrate." Not only that, they find it hard to delineate between students' performances and the teachers' affection for there participation in class.

To treat children as if they already were what they potentially could be requires a special kind of faith—a belief in things hoped for. It is not enough to hope that our children will succeed in their academic, social, and personal lives; we must believe that it will be so. Parents and teachers must take inventory and comprehend whether their communication conveys faith—not just once in a while, but all the time.

God only knows how much I would love to be able to say, "I am an expert at treating my son with such faith 100 percent of the time." The truth is I am not. None of us are. I do try to remain conscious of putting forth my faith in my son and his potential through my actions and my words. Fortunately, there have been occasions when I conveyed optimism and confidence in his future, even when I doubted it myself. I would typically say, "Jim, I believe in you, and God believes in you."

I loved telling stories before bedtime to my two children. My intention was to leave the day on a positive note regardless of what had happed in the course of the day. "Dad!" Jim would sometimes exclaim, "Do you think I will pass all my grades?" The question usually followed a poor school performance or one of his teacher's lectures about putting forth too little effort. At those times, one of my favorite responses included, "Jim, there is no doubt in my mind that God is preparing you for great and mighty things. Don't let anyone—even me—ever steal that thought from you." I would also say, "Jim, there is a season for every garden. Be patient and know that season shall come to you." I never knew if Jim fully understood these words. I knew, though, his spirit was comforted by the underlying faith in him as he drifted off to sleep murmuring, "O.K. Dad, I love you."

Parents and teachers must take inventory of their personal values and find ways to convey a faith in their children regardless of what meets the eye. We all know the popular phrase, "Don't judge a book by its cover." Let's learn to resist showing children strictly where they are in their present performance. Let's learn to show them where they are going without discriminating among past, present, and future performances. Then, children's pursuits of happiness and achievement will ride on the coattails of their increased feelings of acceptance and their beliefs in a brighter and more positive future. This acceptance and power of capability thinking is aligned with Hazel Markus who used the term "Possible Selves" to highlight the importance of such thinking. Markus and Nurris (1986) suggested that people are helped when they see more clearly what they might become in the future. Hock, Schumaker, and Deshler (2003) created strategies designed to nurture such possible selves. The authors recommended that students discover their strengths and weaknesses, identify their hopes, expectations, and fears, plan ways for reaching their goals, and outline methods for working toward their goals. According to the authors, such strategies can become springboards for increasing self-acceptance, nurturing motivation, and heightening expectations.

SUCCESS STRATEGY #2
Develop UNITY Among Parents, Siblings, and Teachers

As if things are not complicated enough for a parent trying to maneuver through the day with struggling learners, it is made harder by the different temperaments and personalities of family members. Often, family members have needs and demands that don't easily take a second or third seat to the needs of a child with learning problems. As a result, conflict ensues, with parents and siblings often experiencing feelings ranging from rejection and abandonment to envy and jealousy. Silver (1998) is right to proclaim, "When one member of a family suffers, everyone in the family feels the pain and reacts to it, sometimes with nearly equal distress"(153).While such reactions may reflect normalcy, they must not be ignored.

Spousal relationships. Spousal friction is not uncommon in households with struggling learners. The addition of children with learning problems to households causes the level of tension, conflict, and frustration to rise. In some instances, wives walk on pins and needles because husbands cannot face the challenging detours caused by learning problems. In other circumstances, husbands and wives have very different views about handling the many issues requiring special attention that arise. This is especially true when different levels of understanding exist about etiology and treatment.

Husbands and wives must take inventory and attend to the health of their relationship with each other. It is hard for two people living in a strained relationship to provide a healthy environment for their children. Children who struggle in school can require tremendous energy from parents, causing much frustration and anxiety. Sometimes, it can be too much for parents whose own relational needs go unmet. It becomes paramount that spouses make emotional deposits to one another. The emotional deposits may include mini-trips without the children, tag-team efforts during homework time, a delineation and division of household responsibilities, and daytime calls to one another to reaffirm affection. More important, spouses must consider their similarities and differences regarding their values about the children's treatment plans, especially for the children whose square pegs fit poorly into the round holes.

What makes it all work? Good communication. Open and ongoing discussions about denial, grieving, goal setting, anger, guilt, learning expectations, expressions of happiness, school, and sibling rivalries and concerns are necessary for survival. This is especially true with sibling issues. Otherwise, parents will find a house divided, where siblings compete for a piece of the attention and inevitably build resentment toward those who appear to acquire the most.

Sibling relationships. Even as an adult, and an older adult at that, I continue to work at demonstrating patience, tolerance, self-control, and unconditional love toward the three other Cooper siblings. Yet, for some reason we expect siblings to master such character skills at an early age. This is unreasonable. All siblings have similar needs—love and affection. Looking through a sibling's eyes, this is usually measured by the quantity of time the sibling receives from his/her parent. Siblings can easily feel neglected when parents of struggling learners spend long hours helping one child stay afloat. This in turn creates animosity toward both the parent and the sibling receiving so much attention.

Unfortunately, there is no real replacement for how much time parents spend, or don't spend, with their children. There are not always enough hours in a day or week to spend equal time with all their children. Single-parent households are especially vulnerable to such challenges. An eleven-year-old girl lamented, "Mom spends all of her time with my sister. My sister has trouble in school. I guess I should start having trouble and maybe Mom would spend more time with me." To an eleven-year-old, this solution makes sense. In an effort to reframe the amount of time the mom spent with her daughter, I advised her to label the moments they spent together as "mom/daughter" time. The following week, the daughter expressed more happily, "Mom is spending so much more time with me." While mom related that the amount of time they spent together hadn't changed, the fact that there now was a special word for that designated time made the union more meaningful and obvious. As mom noted, "It's like highlighting our time together in bold, black capital letters." She was right. Time must be arranged for all children, and it must stand out as something special.

Of course, parent/child time is necessary but not sufficient for resolving tension that often emerges among siblings with and without disabilities. Meyer and Vadasy (1994) suggest workshops for siblings of children with special needs. The workshops called "Sibshops" seek to provide siblings with opportunities for peer support through lively, recreational contexts that emphasize a kids'-eye-view. The authors encourage discussions among siblings of children with special needs about common joys and concerns. These siblings learn how to handle situations commonly experienced by other siblings of children with special needs. The siblings also learn more about the implications of their brothers' and sisters' special needs.

In addition to the time parents devote to siblings with and without disabilities as well as structured activities designed to promote understanding and acceptance among siblings, parents must consider their attitudes about the disabilities. For instance, Seligman (1991) forewarns that children's views are often extensions of their parents' views. Subsequently, the children's ability to accept the disability and cope with the hardship is largely influenced by parental attitude.

Teacher relationships. Teachers are not exempt from the need to appraise the home environment. Combat boots are sometimes necessary when teachers face divisions within households. A common conflict involves parents disagreeing about the question, "What level of pressure is too much?" The wrath of one parent usually results in the other parent taking an opposite approach. In the meantime, teachers sometimes feel like they are being torn in two by the pull from each side.

Cooper and Mosley (1999) suggest that a blind allegiance to the importance of parent involvement causes more harm than good to struggling learners. Therefore, teachers should approach each family's situation cautiously. Asking intense parents to help their children with homework may add fuel to a flame. Parents who struggle with low frustration tolerance are not the best candidates to prepare their children for spelling examinations. How often have teachers been asked, "Why can't my child remember the spelling words from one hour to the next?" Just as there are warning labels on medicine containers, teachers should consider warning labels for parent involvement that say, "The involvement of some parents may be hazardous to the health of their children."

The Bradley's were prime examples of the dangers of involvement. While their hearts were in the right place, their ability to manage their emotions was not. The Bradleys had seven- and eleven-year-old daughters, both with severe learning problems. Of the two, Sarah processed information more slowly than her sister. Dad insisted that his two daughters respond immediately to his commands. Mom wanted more than anything for her daughters to be just like she was.

I will never forget my first encounter with these parents. Dad began, "I am sick and tired of Sarah not doing as I say when I say it. She just looks at me with disrespect. I got spankings for that kind of behavior when I was a boy." Mom jumped, "This is what I put up with all the time. It's like I have three children instead of a husband and two children. I can't get Dad to be more patient." "Patient!" the husband retorted abrasively. "I'm patient enough! You want me to give them a dozen chances. That's why we spend three to four hours every night doing homework, because of all those chances. "Three to four hours?" I asked too quickly. An alarm went off in my head that provoked my counterpunch. "When do the girls get to enjoy the evening?" "Enjoy, hell," the dad barked as his frustration began to surface more and more freely. "Nobody enjoys anything in this family. All we do is work on the girls' homework."

I was not surprised to get little input when I spoke with the two girls. They were immobilized by the fear of expressing feelings within the home. The teacher had no clue that sending schoolwork home with the girls was like placing a missile in their backpack, set for detonation that evening.

Teachers' involvement in sibling issues presents an entirely different challenge. One such problem emerged when our son, the square peg trying to fit in the teacher's round hole, was compared to our daughter, the round peg who fit perfectly in the teacher's round hole. The teacher's expectations were very high for Jim. It was not long before her disappointment became despair. Jim was not the puzzle piece the teacher expected or wanted. His teacher's verbal shot heard around our world was, "I am afraid your son's achievement scores may lower my class average." The accomplishments of one sibling should not be the yardstick used to measure the brother or sister. Teachers must celebrate all children, regardless of their characteristics, and resist forecasting a child's capacity on the basis of family ties.

I received a call one evening from a teacher friend who seemed unusually frantic. "Mark, I made a terrible mistake." I had never heard this very compassionate teacher sound so desperate. "What's happened?" I asked. She cried, "A student of mine overheard me comparing her to her big sister. I know she heard me. I tried to talk with her, but she would have nothing to do with me. Now, what do I do?"

At the least, the teacher needed some tools to repair the problem. While there were many tools that could have helped her, the most important one was to change her attitude. Comparisons among siblings do not belong in the classroom any more than they do in the living room. Siblings don't bring the same qualities to a classroom; this is a fact, one that merits appreciation and celebration, not ratings and comparison.

My friend chose to do the most obvious thing: she admitted her mistake. She told the girl a story about two people. One of them was blind, yet could see and appreciate people perfectly. The other had perfect vision, but saw nothing. The younger sibling loved the story because it acknowledged the teacher's willingness to open her eyes and see more clearly the wonderful qualities of this little girl.

SUCCESS STRATEGY #3
Teach Children the Three Cs—Capable, Connected, Contributing

Career day was an annual event in the high school in our hometown, to which the local residents came to discuss their vocations. I was invited to visit with high school students interested in the teaching profession. As I walked into the room, I recognized many of the young high school students greeting the invited guests. They handed each guest an events program and were also responsible for escorting the guests to different rooms in the school. Most of these students were members of the student council, drill team, athletic program, or cheerleading squad. As I entered the room, I heard a familiar voice call out, "Hi, Dr. Cooper." "Eric, shhh," a teacher responded.

Eric lived just down the street from our home and played with our son on weekends. Although he had disabilities, he never felt any reason to hide from me in the neighborhood. We always encouraged him to communicate and interact just as freely as the other neighborhood friends. Eric was excited as I walked toward him, and I was excited for Eric. I just knew he had a part to play in the career day activities. But before I had a chance to congratulate Eric, the teacher jumped between us, profusely apologizing for Eric's outburst. "Outburst?" I laughed. "Oh, I know Eric from our neighborhood. He and my son are good friends. I'm so glad to see him here." At that moment, the teacher turned and again chastised Eric, "Shhh! I told you to be quiet." Her look and tone of voice erased the beaming smile I had previously seen on Eric's face. He went from the enthusiastic young man I knew around the neighborhood to a student whose teacher thought should be seen and not heard.

Just as the meeting was about to begin, I noticed that Eric and twelve other classmates were paraded out of the cafeteria. My heart sank as Eric and I gazed at one another. I knew then that Eric and his fellow classmates were headed for their special education class. His excitement diminished, and so was my enthusiasm to participate in the career day ceremony. Just before he left my view, he turned, raised his hand, and said, "Bye, Dr. Cooper!" A sense of relief crossed my mind. I thought, "Eric's spirit may be down, but it hasn't been extinguished." Eric defied that teacher's "Shhh!" with his last breath before we lost sight of each other. He was right—his voice was important, too, and on that day; his voice was heard.

What were the values of that school? What message was that teacher sending, with her repeated and stern disapproval of Eric's natural behaviors? It rang out loudly for all to hear: these children don't belong with the rest of the students, they're incapable, they're separate, somehow less than the rest.

"The three Cs," I murmured to myself. Linda Albert (1996) introduced the importance of the three Cs in her book, *Cooperative Discipline.* Albert suggested that children seek to satisfy the three Cs through either appropriate or inappropriate behaviors. It becomes our responsibility as adults, to facilitate the more constructive method of fulfillment. I have encouraged my prospective teachers to use the three Cs as a telling way to measure their effectiveness!

- Do all your students have opportunities to feel CAPABLE?
- Do all your students have opportunities to feel CONNECTED?
- Do all your students have opportunities to CONTRIBUTE?

I was saddened by the experience in the cafeteria that day. The 'shhh' was no whisper. It reverberated in every corner of my mind and heart. I could imagine the 'shhh' meaning, "Eric, leave Dr. Cooper alone. Don't bother him." What stopped the teacher from paying closer attention to Eric's need to feel capable and connected? What stopped the teacher from using this occasion to provide Eric an opportunity to contribute? What stopped anyone from seeing the need to include Eric and his classmates as schoolmates? I guess his developmental disability disqualified him from those opportunities, as if his basic needs were different from those of the other students. There was no question Eric could have stood with the drill team and student council members, the cheerleaders, and athletes to pass out programs. He could have walked with those same high school students to assist the visitors to their respective classes.

That school failed the three Cs. There was no reason for Eric to miss such a wonderful occasion to feel capable. Further, it would have given Eric and the other high school classmates a chance to rub shoulders and connect. Finally, it would have given this young man a chance to contribute to the student body.

Individualized education programs usually address academic growth and development. Many learning expectations require that teachers value knowledge building and skill enhancement in their students. The major focus is on children's ability to read fluently, write masterfully, and compute accurately. Fewer learning expectations are designed to ensure that children with special needs leave school with a sense of capability or connectedness to the student body. Even fewer learning expectations are designed to ensure that children with special needs have opportunities to contribute to school functions. When was the last time you observed children with developmental disabilities, autism, and the like, on the drill team or cheerleading squad or participating on the student council? Valuing the social and emotional growth and development of children is every bit as important as is valuing academic prowess.

Parents and teachers must pay close attention to and evaluate the values of the school environment. Using the three Cs as a measuring tape simplifies such assessment. Children are either experiencing the three Cs or they are not. In experiencing the three Cs, children should be afforded equal opportunity. Equal opportunity is not possible if we fail to seize those occasions where all children can feel capable and connected and where all children can contribute. If those opportunities must be legislated through individualized education programs, then waste no time. This is an important way to ensure that children with special needs are treated with respect, dignity, and optimism. The school system must value the potential of every learner, and this valuing must reflect confidence in all learners.

SUCCESS STRATEGY #4

Teach the Rewards and Dividends of Effort

How do children explain their own performance? Children's answers to this question speak volumes about their view of their abilities. Their responses can tell you much about their present and, very possibly, future motivations. They can also tell much about teachers' and parents' perceptions since most children's views reflect those of the adults. Children and adults usually explain the results of performance in one of the following four ways:

- Effort accounts for performance
- Ability accounts for performance
- Task accounts for performance
- Luck accounts for performance

Dorothy Rich (1992) wrote in *Megaskills,* "The value of believing in effort over native ability is that you can help children do something about their level of effort. It's fatalistic and harder to help them do something about their level of ability. Ability seems set in stone; effort can be influenced; it's open to change" (53). If children attribute their performance to effort, then they believe success is due to their hard work and failure is due to their lack of effort. If they attribute their performance to ability, they believe success is due to their high ability and failure is due to their low ability. If they attribute their performance to task factors, they believe success occurred because the task was easy and failure resulted because the task placed unreasonable demands on their current level of thinking/knowledge. Finally, if they attribute their performance to luck, they believe success reflects their good luck and failure their bad luck.

Ideally, children should attribute success to their efforts, since this is the area they can most easily control, whereas the other explanations—ability, task, and luck—are all out of the children's control. Unfortunately, many children with learning problems are much more inclined to believe that their achievements—or lack thereof—reflect low ability. Children who believe they can control their destinies are more inclined to work harder. However, children who attribute their success to effort are often children who may work hard and still gain limited results, especially when compared to others.

Remember the spoon story I related earlier in the book? It's pertinent here, too. Two men are digging holes. One man is given a spoon to use, while the other is given a shovel. Both men can attribute their success or failure to their efforts; they each have a tool. However, the man with the spoon may be inclined to give up sooner because the payoff for his efforts is minimal, compared to the other guy.

The same happens in school. There are children with learning problems who must work ten times harder than others to get the same grades, yet they receive very little reward comparatively speaking. "I'm tired of trying so hard for so little," Michelle cried one evening. Michelle's parents wanted me to nudge her forward with some encouraging words like, "You can do it!" Although Michelle was used to such encouragement from her parents, they thought that my reinforcement of their words might help. Michelle's frustrated response was, "I KNOW I can do it; that's not the point. I'm tired of working so hard and so long to get things done; it's just not fair. It doesn't take my friends this long, and they still get better grades than I do." Michelle had a great point.

How can we help struggling learners like Michelle combat thoughts of hopelessness like this? Daily, these students face inner voices that repeat, "I'll never measure up with my lack of ability" or "I'm too stupid to do this!"

First, we must help students understand the importance of effort. To do this, we must take the highlighter or magnifying glass off the word "ability" and place more attention on the actions of our students. While they may not be able to consciously articulate this, students view ability as permanent and absolute: You either have it or you don't. They fail to see how anything can change their ability. Struggling learners quickly deduce that students who make the highest grades with the least amount of effort are the most able learners and go on to use these students as measuring sticks for their own abilities. What they fail to understand is that ability is not, in itself, the key to success. Effort is the key! But children cannot and will not change their views until teachers and parents change their thinking on such matters and reinforce effort as much as, or more than, outcome.

Second, teachers and parents must help struggling learners shift their attention from an obsession with ability to an emphasis on the task at hand. A simple yet effective way to do this is to make accomplishment albums, where children document their accomplishments using a diary, a collage, and/or a photo album. Michelle's teacher encouraged her to convert a photo album to an accomplishment album. Gradually, Michelle began to take pride in the daily review of her accomplishments; they became akin to notches on her belt. In fact, Michelle brought her accomplishment album to my office and eagerly exclaimed, "Look at what I've done in just a week's worth of work!"

Third, Children must not only learn the value of effort, but also to treat time as a friend. Making time a bosom buddy was difficult for Michelle. She was the student using the spoon while her classmates used shovels, backhoes, and bulldozers. I spent time talking to Michelle about famous people and also unfamiliar people whose roads to success took a little longer than others. Over time Michelle became less and less self-conscious about the amount of time she spent on tasks compared to others.

Finally, we must help children with learning problems see themselves as capable learners. Children who see themselves as capable are more inclined to make future attempts to learn because of their prior learning experiences. Parents and teachers can facilitate this thinking in a number of ways. One, children tend to see themselves as capable learners when they see others with similar backgrounds learn effectively. Expose them to these people, either in person or through books or stories. Two, children need a lot of encouragement about their competence. Give it to them! Three, children need specific feedback about their efforts. It is not enough to say, "Good job!" Be specific. "Michelle, I can tell you are taking more initiative in your studies. I saw you working independently on two occasions. That initiative will help you complete the math problems more successfully in the future." Four, children can better see themselves as capable learners if they take one day at a time. Again, the accomplishments albums can help here. And, lastly, help students distinguish between having ability and being capable.

In Michelle's case, an analogy did the trick. I asked, "Michelle, why would you want to keep a cap on your head?" Michelle laughed and said, "It'd help you hide your bald head." Following her humorous response, with which she was quite pleased, she added, "It helps keep you warm in cold weather." I then asked that she look carefully at the word "capable." She noticed the two words, cap and able. I suggested that she keep the "cap" on "able" just as a person keeps a cap on his or her head to keep warm. This seemed to click for Michelle. She began to realize the difference between capable and ability, that ability involved the now and felt more permanent whereas capable involved the future and felt changeable.

The bottom line is that children's own values are deciding factors in their quests for success. What we, as parents and teachers, can do is to increase their propensity to attribute success to effort versus luck, ability, or task. We can also inspire children to see intelligence as something that can change with effort. Finally, we can influence children's views of their learning capacities.

This being the case, the natural temptation is for parents and teachers to sacrifice everything to help their children achieve success. In doing so we often maximize children's efforts and accomplishments while diminishing their experiences. This brings us to Strategy #5, an important companion to #4 and one that must be integrated into the overall strategy plan for a child.

SUCCESS STRATEGY #5
Replace the Three Rs with Leisure, Caring, and Versatility

Most children with learning challenges have few opportunities to smell the roses. The same goes for their well-meaning parents, who often come up for air hyperventilating over their efforts to master reading, writing, and arithmetic. There seems to be no other way but study, study, and more study. Those who try to break from schoolwork on an intermittent basis have trouble justifying the more restful, leisurely activities.

There must be time to smell the roses. All work and no play do not keep failure at bay. There is no scientific evidence that says, "The more our children perform schoolwork, the better they will do." A point of no return is reached when children are satiated with academic demands. It is a point we must learn to recognize and respect. Children with learning problems are children first. Their hearts and minds need a reprieve from the daily struggle toward success. They need diversion and rest through leisure activities, caring opportunities, and experiences designed to teach versatility.

Teachers can be instrumental in conveying this strategy to parents. They have a choice; they can communicate a myopic vision that suggests that the mastery of skills is the only road to success. Or, they can convey a calmness that says, "Maturation, time, experience, and attitude are wonderful catalysts for your child's future success. Don't place all your eggs in basket of academic skills." Prevailing educational standards suggest that children who perform "best" in school are those who excel in the verbal-linguistic and logic-mathematical areas. There are many other areas where children can excel once we exit from this tunnel view. Teachers must help parents understand that children need more than just academics to be happy and whole. They must encourage their children to explore areas outside their academic deficits and appreciate that a variety of other qualities contribute to health, happiness, and healing.

Leisure. A thirteen-year-old girl with learning problems visited my office with her dad. The young girl had a particular complaint about her father. While she appeared somewhat apologetic for blaming her dad for the problem, nevertheless she complained, "My dad spends very little time with me." Her dad wasted no time protesting, "I am constantly spending time with you. We do schoolwork every night for at least two hours."

Yes, dad spent time with his daughter, but it was not the kind of time his daughter craved. Luckily, dad was amenable to the idea that leisure time was as important as academics and homework. Together, they decided soccer was a way to enjoy their relationship outside the laborious activity called schoolwork. It did not take long before dad and daughter began to enjoy one another's company again. This renewed spirit of loving and liking spilled over and improved the quality of their relationship while performing schoolwork.

There are other reasons why leisure activities are so important. Leisure time provides an opportunity for positive emotions to surface. Often, the leisure activity reinforces children's natural strengths and abilities. In this instance, the daughter liked soccer because she could perform without ridicule and embarrassment.

Leisure for my son, Jim, was a quality meal at a fine restaurant. Because the environment was so enjoyable to him, this leisure activity became an opportunity for me to initiate more serious conversations. An outing to a restaurant was often an incentive for him to address challenging questions such as, "What plans can we make to improve your homework completion rate during the next six weeks?" Of course, most conversations should leave school-related matters on the backburner. Fisher and Cummings (1995) encouraged, "While it's necessary to spend some time on school-related matters, it's equally important to relax with your child, whether you are reading, playing, talking, or just sitting quietly together" (86). Parents should resist becoming so consumed by the struggles that the more enjoyable times diminish from sight and sound. The relationship building that occurs during leisure time allows for a more peaceful discussion about school matters.

Caring. John Maxwell (1997), one of the leading experts in the area of personal and corporate leadership and author of *The Success Journey,* highlighted the value of service to others when he cited Winston Churchill's quote, "We make a living by what we get, but we make a life by what we give (p. 17)." Children with learning challenges spend an inordinate amount of time getting an education. While we all understand the value of an education, school reflects, perhaps more than anything else we do in our lives, our frailties, ineptness, and deficiency. How many adults would remain compliant when told, "O.K. folks, let's spend six hours per day for the next twelve years working on projects that appear Greek to us." Not many. Children are no different, except for their propensity to remain more compliant and less assertive about their dissatisfaction.

Education is what we get. We create our quality of life by what we learn to give. Helping others does not require the same knowledge and skills as academics do. Helping others can be very reinforcing considering the positive feedback that usually accompanies acts of caring. By sowing seeds that will help others, children learn to help themselves in profound ways. First, they experience positive self-image thoughts. They can say to themselves, "Look what I can do and look how much what I do is appreciated." Second, they exercise relational muscles that connect them with others. Many children with learning problems feel like chronic receivers. They need opportunities to feel like givers too to bring balance and a sense of belonging to their lives.

I saw this lifeline develop with Benjamin. He was a boy who continued to ignore his schoolwork assignments and saw his grades slipping dramatically as a result. He had decided that he was not good enough to complete the assignments successfully. In fact, he insisted, "There's nothing I can do good!" Benjamin's attitude changed when his parents connected him with a coach who needed someone to take care of the team's balls, bats, and other tasks. Once he got involved, Benjamin's caring could not be turned off. He not only provided water for the players, he reorganized the schedule for water breaks so that it reflected outdoor temperatures. As the players started noticing Benjamin's commitment to them, many began to show a similar level of commitment to him. Finally, Benjamin experienced something he could do successfully. His success had little to do with what he gained or accomplished. It reflected what he did for others.

Versatility. Mom was closely involved with my growth and development. She was the rock upon which I could rely for help and encouragement. I never heard Mom second-guess her participation with one exception. A few years ago she commented, "If I had an opportunity to do it all over again, I would have created more opportunities for you to learn about art, music, and other areas that would have made you more versatile as a person."

I must agree with her reflection. The greatest challenge I presently face is my lack of versatility. While I long for a greater breadth of knowledge in more areas, such as art, music, and geography, I invest too little time in such activities. I have spent my life being a jack-of-few-trades instead of a jack-of-all-trades.

There is a fine line separating the two. If children place too much emphasis on becoming a jack-of-all-trades, they may become a jack-of-no-trades because developing a trade takes so much energy, effort, and practice. At the same time, children who place all their eggs in one basket run the risk of becoming less versatile compared to children exposed to more knowledge across more disciplines. Often, the excitement of learning new and different information renews the spirit of learning and makes the academic learning more tolerable and sometime more effective and efficient.

Strategy #5 asks you to see the world around your child in a different light, to define it in terms that reflect the needs of the whole child. It suggests that there is more to life than just academics. Teaching our children how to take breaks to enjoy leisure activities, to demonstrate acts of kindness, and learn things outside school requirements is not always easy. Making it even more difficult is the hurried mentality among parents and teachers that often suggests that there is too little time to do it all.

As we move into Strategy #6, we see that parents and teachers who treat time as a scarce commodity usually believe that the child's performance is a reflection of their own performance—good or bad. Strategy #6 addresses this thinking and suggests ways for parents and teachers to resist the temptation to make children's performance their own problem.

SUCCESS STRATEGY #6

Separate Children's Performances from the Perception of Parent and Teacher Performances

I began seeing Mr. and Mrs. Conrad's two children when one was beginning third grade and the other the fifth grade. Both children were diagnosed with learning disabilities severe enough to require many modifications within the home and school environments. In this case however, the severity of the problem was more a reflection of the parents' attitudes, especially those of Mrs. Conrad.

Mrs. Conrad had many wonderful memories of her childhood. She talked about being on the cheerleading squad, student council, and girls' basketball team. She excelled academically, and was warmly accepted by her male counterparts, as she was a very attractive girl. She desperately wanted her daughters to have the same positive experiences. While this attitude is not unusual among parents, the depth of Mrs. Conrad's desire made her children's personal struggles worse. Both her children already labored with schoolwork and were doing their best just to stay afloat. Their challenges were severe enough without the added insistence that they recapture their mom's childhood experiences. Furthermore, Mrs. Conrad was spending most of her time focusing on who they "should" be, without making reasonable attempts to treat her children as if they were what they could be. In her mind, they should be great athletes, accomplished students, beauty queens, and leaders—everything she had experienced during school.

Mrs. Conrad identified much too strongly with the failure of her children to achieve her own personal notions of the meaning of success. When the children failed, so did she. Other parents are affected in a different way by their children's performances. Theo was a five-year-old who never sat still and manifested many episodes of opposition. This was an escalating problem, especially when his behaviors surfaced at church, the grocery store, or other public places like restaurants. Theo was a child who expressed, "I want what I want when I want it!" While visiting with the mom and dad, I asked the mom, "How are you doing?" This simple question opened the floodgates within seconds. She wept for a couple of minutes before saying, "Nobody has ever asked. I feel so ashamed, guilty, and embarrassed all the time. I just know people look at me and wonder what's wrong with me. My son's behavior makes me feel so inadequate." At that moment, dad placed his arm around his wife noting, "For the longest time, I left the child rearing to my wife. I began to help when I noticed Theo running all over my wife. I figured he needed a man's hand. I found out rather quickly what a hard time my wife was having." The mom interrupted, "Just the other day, a lady in the grocery store asked if I had ever heard of whippings. I just wish that lady could spend one day with my child."

Parents are not the only people who align personally with children's struggles. Theo's teacher expressed a similar sentiment. "I am so mad at Theo for not behaving better in class. I get sick and tired of nursing him at the expense of spending less time with the other students." I probed: "What makes you so incensed?" She insisted, "It's not fair to the other children when I spend so much time fighting with Theo. It's just not fair." "Is there anything that Theo's behavior says about you?" I asked. Tears began to fall and she openly wept while exclaiming, "I am so mad because he makes me feel incapable. Until now, I thought I would be a good teacher." This little five-year-old who ruled the roost in the classroom had visibly shaken his teacher's confidence. It did not help that a percentage of her colleagues brutalized her with statements such as, "You need to just get stern with the child and everything will work out fine."

Parents and teachers must guard against taking children's performances personally. In most instances, struggling learners are not struggling because of adult inadequacy. This does not mean that adults do not play an important role. It means that adults are not the cause of the struggles, but they are critical parts of the solution. Once parents and teachers separate their egos from the children's performances, they are more inclined to find solutions that fulfill Success Strategy #7 and they begin to magnify children's abilities while minimizing their inabilities.

SUCCESS STRATEGY #7
Magnify Children's Skills and Minimize Their Deficits

The hotel room felt very small, but I was aware that the claustrophobic feelings were due more to the situation I was in than the size of the room. Sitting opposite me were three faculty members interviewing me for their Ph.D. program in early childhood education. Actually, I was handling the intense grilling pretty well until the question I had dreaded was finally asked. It was a question that shadows many people affected by learning challenges: "How are you going to perform at the Ph.D. level with your unsatisfactory G.R.E. score?"

"Here we go again," I thought. "We are smart enough to place a man on the moon, but we are not smart enough to understand that the combination of intellect, creativity, tenacity, determination, and effort has more to do with performance than a G.R.E. score."

The three faculty members waited while I composed my reply. "The G.R.E. speaks to my deficits. It has little to do with my strengths. My previous and present accomplishments reflect my ability to think, create, analyze, and comprehend." I was not only proud of my statement, I was also proud of the delivery. There was not a crack in my voice, a flinch of my fingers, or a blink of an eye. The ball was now on their side of the court. A faculty member continued, "How do you anticipate doing in three statistics courses and the advanced measurement class? They are all requirements. Are you sure that your G.R.E. score is not an indication of your inability to perform well in those courses?" With a smoothness that surprised me, I countered, "The intangibles in my mind, heart, and spirit are far greater than a number depicted by a standardized examination. I am an accomplished author, speaker, and teacher. I know how to influence people, and I care as much or more than anybody about the people I influence. I do not consider myself a high risk. All I want is the chance to demonstrate what I have already demonstrated in other areas." Once I finished, I felt a deep sense of relief. I had said what needed to be said; the outcome was now in their hands. They could let a G.R.E. score influence their decision or use a combination of my experiences, accomplishments, and determination to decide. Fortunately, they chose *me*.

Parents and teachers must emphasize children's strengths instead of magnifying their weaknesses. School represents but a small capsule in the lives of struggling learners. Furthermore, it often measures a minute part of children's abilities. How else can we explain why thousands of people who score high on examinations fail to do well in life and many thousands of people who perform poorly achieve greatness?

Struggling learners should not be subjected to the myopic vision that requires precision testing where examinations are designed to zero in on deficits or weaknesses. Precision testing is like precision bombing. The military bombs select specific targets in hopes of removing the enemy rather than killing the innocent. Precision testing involves the examination bombs designed to identify specific weaknesses. Unlike military bombs, these examination bombs do not remove the enemy—deficit test scores. In many instances, they highlight the deficits at the expense of targeting children's strengths. Society needs to discover and maximize the potential of all learners. This cannot occur by minimizing their opportunities through precision testing.

At one point in my professional life I was following the school career of a student who continued to demonstrate weaknesses on standardized examinations and the precision testing conducted in her school. She often shared her trials and tribulations with me because of my ability to identify with the prejudices and biases that occur with struggling learners. One particular year she complained, "Why do schools try so hard to discourage rather than encourage? Why do schools magnify what I can't do rather than what I can? Why do schools think they can teach better through failure than success?" I could sense her feelings of growing resignation and hostility. I could not help but think about my own experiences and the interview about my G.R.E. score. I thought to myself, "If people who score so high on standardized examinations are so smart, why is it that some of them act so dumb?"

Parents and teachers must develop their own strategic missile defense mechanism, one designed to prevent the examination bombs from detonating in the minds and hearts of children with learning problems. Parents and grandparents have always forewarned that we keep away from people who try to belittle our abilities. This is easier said than done, especially when some of the people who belittle their abilities do so through testing. It becomes the job of parents and teachers to watch for such situations. If we don't, our children with learning disabilities will give up or will spend the rest of their lives looking for affirmation and acceptance through the false prophet called testing.

Our daily mantra should become: the whole is greater than the sum of its parts. We must not ourselves, nor let anyone else, judge our children on the basis of one score when there are multitudes of contributing qualities that bear witness to their strengths. Success strategy #8 involves one of these contributing qualities as children learn to use their mental and emotional armor as a weapon against examination piety.

SUCCESS STRATEGY #8

Help your Children Compensate for Their Challenges with Mental and Emotional Armor

Children who process information slowly may need more time to complete assignments or take exams. Children who have organization problems may need an organizer to help them record expectations and requirements. Children who have trouble taking notes effectively may need to use a tape recorder. Children who read poorly may need a taped text. Often children with some form of learning disabilities are given physical tools to help them compensate. That is, recognize the need and respond with an appropriate intervention.

Parents and teachers must also equip children with learning problems with another set of tools: a mental and emotional armor designed to shield them from attacks. Compensation is an effective strategy to help children acquire mental and emotional armor. As used here, compensation means that individuals counterbalance their weaknesses by capitalizing on their strengths. Learning problems can include a wide variety of deficits, such as reading, writing, speaking, listening, computing, coordination, and/or socialization. Rather than children centering their lives on their deficits, parents and teachers must teach them to use their strengths as launching pads. This can only be done if children learn to accept two very important personal characteristics—deficits and strengths.

Children who learn to accept their deficits learn not only that there is something to overcome, but also that they can go beyond their present level of functioning. People who fail to acknowledge their deficits have little reason to counterbalance them. Their contentment may facilitate happiness, yet there is little forward movement. For instance, children are less inclined to demonstrate tenacity when they see no need to be persistent with a topic or subject. Children's perception of their deficiencies can become the mental and emotional energy that propels them off the launching pad.

Children's acceptance of their deficits is not enough; we must teach them what to do with the deficits once they recognize they exist. Several years ago, my wife's aunt went through a battle with cancer. Given three to five years to live, Nell not only accepted dying, she used her acceptance as a launching pad for living. Nell exclaimed, "I plan to make memories!" And memories are what Nell made along with everyone else whose lives she touched. Parents and teachers must help children take measures to reframe their thinking about the deficiencies in more positive and constructive terms.

Successful compensation involves one more action: children learning to accept their strengths. Because school provides so many reminders of their deficits, it is typically much harder for struggling learners to recognize and embrace their strengths. Parents and teachers must be vigilant in their efforts to help children identify their strengths. How else can children counterbalance their deficits?

Measures must be taken to help cultivate strengths among children with learning problems. This starts by recognizing that there are different kinds of strengths to cultivate. Some strengths reflect children's natural abilities. Whether it's sports, music or art, children thus inclined can draw tremendous strength from their talents and thus counterbalance their deficits with such qualities, if appreciated.

Other strengths require a more in-depth cultivation. They reside in the inner realm, and include strengths such as tenacity, determination, delayed gratification, resisting temptation, patience, persistence, perseverance, and risk-taking. Some children have temperaments and personalities that naturally include these critical strengths. In most children they need to be brought forth if the children are to survive the trials and tribulations of learning problems. This often requires that parents and teachers devote an extraordinary amount of time encouraging such attitudes and behaviors. The efforts of these caring adults are rewarded when children begin to recognize these inner strengths as important tools with which to overcome their learning challenges.

Ross was a perfect example of a child who needed to recognize his deficits and strengths. His parents and teacher had asked me to help Ross become more independent and less demanding. They believed that Ross failed to utilize his strengths.

The day I met him he was sitting in a wheelchair paying close attention to his elementary school teacher. Ross had been told to expect a man to visit with him that day. I entered the room and walked toward Ross's seat. While he was aware of my presence, Ross did not make any eye contact with me. I introduced myself and explained the purpose of my visit. Following a several-second pause, Ross looked at me and made a grunting noise as if to say, "Well, let's go." However, he made no move toward the door. Moderately confused, I said, "Excuse me?" Ross became agitated and asked more emphatically, "Aren't you taking me somewhere to talk?"

Ross was expecting me to push him. He was used to calling the shots at school and home and ordering people around. To Ross, I was just another handyman. For the moment I obliged, the wheels in my head turning faster than those of his chair. As I pushed Ross down the hall, I started huffing and puffing. He seemed surprised by my behavior, even more so when I stopped, sat down in the middle of the hall, and said, "I'm worn out from pushing you." Ross promptly asked, "Well, how long will you need to rest?" "I'm not sure, but it could be through the lunch period," I responded. Ross expressed astonishment, grunted, and then said, "O.K., I can push myself." Although old habits do not change overnight, this encounter was the beginning of freedom for Ross, his teacher, and his parents. Ross began to recognize his deficits from muscular dystrophy. He also began to appreciate and utilize his strengths. Ross began to compensate and use his mental and emotional armor to fortify him for can-do thinking and actions.

My personal story is another example of inner strength. When tenacity, determination, persistence, and perseverance all became bosom buddies, feelings of resignation, disappointment, and despair waned. As those inner strengths became more muscular through constant exercise, the deficits seemed much weaker and more easily overcome. Parents and teachers should never underestimate the value of tenacity and determination among children. They are wonderful qualities that can compensate for many deficits. While there are many ways to develop such inner strengths as well as the natural strengths, one of the more important ingredients in children's ability to compensate is the tendency to see themselves as being powerful. Success strategy #9 helps parents and teachers empower children to take greater and greater control over their inner and outer resources.

Success Strategy #9
Promote the Empowerment of Children

Early on, children embark on a quest for power. According to William Glasser (1997), a prominent psychiatrist and educational consultant, all of our behavior is our best attempt to control ourselves to meet four basic needs. One such need is power. Glasser suggested that children are usually contented and better behaved when their needs are met, but discontented and often misbehaving when their needs are not being met. Children want to be the boss—of themselves, their parents, their teacher, and sometimes even the whole class. They want to show others "I am in charge and you cannot make me do what I do not want to do." This is especially true among adolescents as they reach a developmental need to put distance between themselves and other adults, especially their parents.

Children with learning problems are caught between a rock and a hard place where power is concerned. On the one hand, like everyone else, they experience the need to establish their own identity, their separateness. On the other hand, they soon find that this distance interferes with other wants and needs, especially those that require help from others, such as completing an assignment, writing a satisfactory paper, and/or preparing successfully for an examination. The anguish these children feel can be severe, as they internally wrestle with the issue "I need you, but I don't want you!"

To start, it's important that parents and teachers understand children's basic need for power and their developmental movement from dependency to independence. It can be a tough road. But take heart! It doesn't have to turn into a battle. Hidden within these power-seeking behaviors is a golden nugget that parents and teachers can cultivate and nurture—leadership.

As Rodney explained his reason for seeing me, the chip on his shoulders grew with every word. "Mom and Dad are making me come here. In fact, they make me do everything I do. They are the biggest bullies in the world!" Rodney had spent eight grades swimming against a strong current while trying to succeed academically. There was no question his success reflected much of his parents' efforts to make him succeed. He was a young man with no voice or no choice. Because there were no legitimate ways for Rodney to receive power, he had started engaging in a variety of both passive and active strategies for seeking power. His passive strategies included avoidance behaviors masked by lying or quiet noncompliance. In Rodney's eyes, his punishment for lying was not nearly as bad as his parents' demand that he complete his work. His quiet behaviors of noncompliance took the form of "O.K., I will do my homework right after I finish watching this commercial." When more actively seeking to exert his power, Rodney engaged in the occasional temper tantrum, loudly claiming that no one cared for him. This latter strategy, he had discovered, usually solicited enough empathy to get him off the hook for whatever he had done.

Rodney's intervention plan included developing a "board" with Rodney as the chairman of the board and his teacher and parents as board members. This strategy gave Rodney both voice and choice. We need to recognize that there is a difference between having one's say and having one's way. Children with learning problems sometimes need their *say* more than their *way*. Most of these children would love to work successfully on their own. However, many will not achieve successfully without help from parents and teachers.

To complete the intervention, I arranged a "board meeting" for Rodney, his parents, and his teacher to discuss Rodney's needs, complete with a hand-picked chair from the principal's office to give him even more clout. Rodney was excited about this opportunity to be in charge of the meeting. Although it was a simple strategy, it granted him legitimate power designed to prevent negative power struggles. It worked perfectly. Rodney began delegating responsibilities to everyone involved, including him. In fact, he became more demanding of himself than were his parents and teacher.

With a little thought and a little investigation, parents and teachers can find all sorts of ways to empower children like Rodney. Pocock et al. (2002) recommended that parents and teachers empower children by promoting self-advocacy, self-awareness, and self-determination. In doing so, leadership skills begin to emerge. According to the authors, children with those leadership skills begin to better understand their own disabilities and how they can affect their educational experiences. In the book, *Raising a Thinking Child Workbook,* Myrna Shure (2000) presented strategies to help children become problem solvers. Shure's recommendations promote a freedom for children to think for themselves. This freedom empowers children not only to solve everyday problems guaranteed for struggling learners, but also to see themselves as the problem solvers. This is far better than seeing themselves as victims or simply as recipients who require others to solve problems for them. The latter is no more than the same old thing where children "need" help due to their inability to provide the necessary help for themselves.

There are simple things we can do to avoid disempowering children. Disempowerment appears in raised voices, in facial-verbal exchanges, in a lack of listening, and in blaming. Empowerment, on the other hand, comes from a willingness by parents, teachers, and children to consider a variety of viewpoints, change the subject when necessary, share responsibility, or stay focused on relevant issues. Sometimes it includes rescheduling a time to meet with cooler heads, or a willingness to table a discussion. Logic must prevail over emotion in order for empowerment and the resistance to disempowerment to occur. There is no worse time to debate decisions than when emotions are high and strong. There is no better way for the chairman of the board and his cabinet to make decisions than when logical thinking and cooler heads prevail.

Once the empowerment of struggling learners becomes an integral part of the educational recipe, best efforts among the learners are maximized and barriers that inhibit the use of children's talent, creativity, and energy are minimized (Fisher & Thomas, 1996). Without such empowerment, children who struggle are more inclined to hold back, give safe responses, and make tentative commitments; all formulas for decreasing the probability of achievement and success.

The final strategy in this chapter outlines some of the many common distortions in thinking that interfere with logical reasoning among parents and teachers. Not only must we learn to recognize these common thought distortions, we must learn how to convert them into logical thoughts.

SUCCESS STRATEGY #10
Manage Thought Distortions

There's one important person in the world who can make you feel despondent or depressed. This same person can also make you feel exuberant, ecstatic, and excited. That person is you! When fully grasped and understood, this simple idea is life changing. Our emotions stem from our thoughts. It's this way for parents, teachers, children, adults, and everyone in between. It's no different for children with learning problems. What is encouraging is that we can help them understand that tremendous changes in their actions are but a thought away.

Looking around, I've noticed that most people are unaware of how their thinking impacts their lives. Many people fall into patterns of thinking that distort reality. In his book, *Ten Days to Self-Esteem*, David Burns (1993) outlined a variety of thought distortions that interfere with one's logic. There are the All-or-nothing thinkers who only see things in black-and-white categories. The Defeatist thinkers view negative events as never-ending patterns that are impossible to change, whereas Negative thinkers dwell only on the negatives to the exclusion of the positives. The Mind Readers know not only their own reality, but also the realities of everyone around them, even when these others don't know them! The Fortune-Tellers make predictions that, once vocalized, they hold as truths resistant to change or reinterpretation. Lastly we encounter people who blow things out of proportion, the Magnifiers, or those who downplay the importance of events, the Minimizers. In each instance, these thought patterns rob us, and those whom we involve, of the wondrous gift we humans possess—our innate ability to recreate ourselves and our situations by just changing our thoughts.

All-or-nothing thinkers. Parents and teachers often suffer from this type of thought distortion when faced with their own imperfections or feelings of inadequacy. Children with learning problems can bring out the worst in some adults. Mrs. Alford once remarked, "I can't do one thing right when I try to help my son complete his homework. We wind up yelling at each other every time. I must be the world's worst parent." Teachers can also fall victim to all-or-nothing thinking. My daughter's teacher considered herself one of the best teachers in her school until my son joined her classroom. Within months, her self-worth went from extremely high to extremely low. The truth was somewhere in between.

Defeatist thinkers. Children who exhibit learning problems at a young age continue manifesting learning problems in some capacity at a later age. This doesn't mean they will never achieve success. Parents and teachers who view the glass as being half empty rather than half full can be heard to say, "This child will never read fluently, calculate accurately, or write masterfully because of his earlier track record." There are far too many examples of children who learned more slowly, or lagged behind who have gone on to accomplish great and mighty things. A teacher once told the internationally acclaimed composer, Beethoven that he was hopeless as a composer. Thomas Edison's teacher said that he was too stupid to learn anything. There are tens of thousands more cases that disprove the argument that a pattern of negative events cannot become positive.

Negative thinkers. The most graphic example of negative thinking that comes to mind is the teacher who labeled one of the children in her class Jeffrey Dahmer because he often bit the teachers and other students. Joshua was a child who spent five hours fifty-nine minutes and forty-eight seconds each day using a safe mouth and only twelve seconds biting. Yet, the biting was all the teacher could see in this boy. Parents and teachers must resist overemphasizing the negative and start thinking about the positive. In Joshua's case, the parents and teachers began to place more emphasis on Joshua's positive behavior. Throughout the day, they were instructed to say, "Oh, I see Joshua using a safe mouth." This shift in thinking and acting transformed Joshua from a boy who bit other children to a boy who played safely with other children. It also resulted in a shift in the teacher's mindsets, as she became more aware of how much of Joshua's time was actually spent demonstrating good behavior. Children with learning problems need parents and teachers who insist on finding the silver lining within their children's daily actions. Positive expectations hasten the process whereby the children's daily actions become more consistent with the positive expectations.

Mind readers. Some parents are sure they know what other people are thinking, especially about their child. They project, "I know the teachers and other parents believe my child is not trying." Sometimes mind reading appears, as "I know they think I'm not trying hard enough to help my child." Mind reading can be dangerous and is usually very destructive, as most often it is rooted in the negative. Parents and teachers must try to eliminate this "know-it-all" mentality. It places undue pressure on parents who already live with enough pressure. Furthermore, the inherent danger in making assumptions is that we usually make them with incomplete information! Most people don't go around with a pen and paper jotting down the myriad details that would be necessary to realistically evaluate the performances of others. Rather than mind-read, parents and teachers can more openly communicate the intention to stay positive. When we view mind reading as an inappropriate method of interacting with our children or the people who work with them, we will naturally cultivate a more stress free and rested mind.

Fortune-tellers. In counseling parents and professionals, I frequently hear comments like, "I just don't think this child will ever accomplish much" or "He'll never be able to keep up with his peers." Many times people are unaware of the extent to which this type of thinking occupies their minds. One certain outcome of this kind of thinking is that it limits the capabilities of many struggling learners. When we limit our thinking, we limit the possibilities we work to create in our lives and those of our children.

Fortune-tellers are pessimists who fail to see the potential in others. There are thousands of stories inside and outside the disability community that reflect people defying all odds and accomplishing much more than their childhood experiences would indicate. It all starts with a belief that there is potential within our children, potential deep and strong enough to get them through the daily struggles they will undoubtedly face. These struggles are hard enough for children with learning disabilities without parents and teachers making predictions of their future failures. If fortune-tellers must practice their trade, we must insist that they stop making negative or limiting predictions about achievement, progress, and success. Otherwise, this type of thinking will invariably run any amount of dedication and resolve a child has directly into nothingness.

Magnifiers and Minimizers. The adage, "Don't make a mountain out of a molehill," has been around for many years. So has, "It's really not that bad." Both of these sentiments describe potentially damaging thought processes. The magnifier makes things seem worse than they really are. For example an F reflects more than a failed grade on a test to parents and teachers who are magnifiers. It reflects FF—future failures. The Magnifier defines the future from the present—not a bad idea if they would also project that same thinking when something positive occurs. But most often this thinking reflects a sense of doom and gloom, with an emphasis on the negative. Children with learning problems are battling with failure from a very early age. They don't need outside reinforcement for such terminal thinking.

On the flip side of the coin are the Minimizers who adhere to a mindset that, while rooted in compassion, can be just as damaging. Parents and teachers often try to insulate and protect children with learning problems from hurt by saying, "I see you got an F. It's no big deal. Don't worry about it." Or they believe that by ignoring the challenges, they will miraculously disappear.

Neither type of thinking is beneficial to a child with learning disabilities. Parents and teachers must curtail their tendencies to minimize situations or blow them out of proportion. A good strategy to keep this type of thinking in check is to always listen. Listen to children express their fears and apprehensions. Listen to your children when they ask for your guidance and emotional support. Then deal with the situation at hand, honestly and realistically. Magnifiers and Minimizers live in the future. Our job as parents and teachers is to help our children NOW. When we view each day as a new opportunity for positive change, we keep alive the idea that tomorrow our children will succeed.

The thought distortions described here can interfere with the best efforts of parents and teachers. When thought distortions are left unchallenged, either through a lack of awareness or a disregard for their power, they become like quicksand to our children's future growth and development. While the consequences may be slow, an inch today, another inch next week, parents, teachers, and children eventually become so deeply buried in the sand that they suffocate with such thinking.

The greatest counterpunch to thought distortions is rational and logical thinking. Parents and teachers must continually ask themselves, "Do my present thoughts make good sense?" "Does history support my present thoughts?" "Is this a pattern or is it an isolated occurrence?" There is always an alternative thought we can substitute in our minds. When parents or teachers say, "You are not going to pass with that F!" they must challenge that distortion with, "Have children who made F's ever passed the grade? Of course they have, by the millions!" To those who suggest, "This struggle will never pass," say, "Yes, it can, and here's how we can make it better."

The ten success strategies outlined in this chapter are not exhaustive of the ways parents and teachers give support and encouragement to struggling learners. They illuminate some of the common, but unhealthy habits we all possess that can negatively affect the lives of children with learning challenges. When practiced on a daily basis, they will resurrect good but forgotten habits, or perhaps help develop new and better habits. One thing is certain. Our pursuit to help children with learning problems cannot be accomplished alone. It requires a collective effort among many people using a multitude of strategies.

Success Strategy #11
Exercise the Six Habits That Teach Life-Abilities/Success Skills

One of the most difficult challenges in working with teachers, parents, and struggling learners is to get all parties working from the same script and the same page. Each party brings his or her own ideas, goals, expectations, hopes and dreams to the collaboration. Most often the result is confusion and motion, but not much movement in helping the challenged student.

Although teachers, parents, and children are working toward the same goal—success—confusion inevitably arises with the question "How do we get to that end?" There are many avenues toward success. Some people encounter only a few valleys, strong currents, or steep mountains. Others need to work hard against stiff winds, walk tight ropes over high cliffs, and contend with landmines at every step. Struggling learners relate most with this latter group. It is critical that we not waste effort, but provide them with a structured game plan that will help minimize the severe challenges and create a fertile path toward success.

Teaching life-abilities or success skills is a critical component of the game plan. It is not just or fair to leave to chance the inculcation of these skills within the lives of our children. They must be taught, exercised and reinforced. Life-abilities or success skills include attentiveness, orderliness, truthfulness, responsibility, effort, problem solving, resilience, common sense, initiative, self-control, resourcefulness, diligence, boldness, thoroughness, determination, persuasiveness, and problem solving. Dorothy Rich (1992) suggested that such abilities or skills are the best gift one can give to children. Devine, Seuk, and Wilson (2001) called them life's most essential goals. Ernest Boyer (1995), author of *The Basic School: A Community for Learning* called them core virtues. I call them life's great equalizers.

Parents, special educators, and general educators must pay close attention to the development of Individual Education Programs that address such abilities and skills that relate to the social and emotional health of children with disabilities. Fletcher-Janzen and De Pry (2003) indicated that national surveys of IEP content indicate that annual goals and behavioral objectives for social competency are rare, even when the student's disability dictates that such goals and objectives need to be included in the IEP. The authors suggested the parents and school personnel develop goals and objectives centered on areas of cooperation, organization, responsibility, and empathy. This suggestion is closely aligned with Goleman's (1995) groundbreaking book entitled *Emotional Intelligence*. Goleman recommended the goal of raising the level of social and emotional competence in children as a part of their regular education—not just something taught remedially to children who are faltering and identified as "trouble," but a set of skills and understandings essential for all children. While Goleman's recommendations address all children, many children with learning disabilities have even greater needs for such social and emotional competence. Subsequently, among families and school educators of struggling learners, there should be no time wasted before embracing the promotion of social and emotional skills.

These skills level the playing field for challenged learners, provide them with tools that facilitate learning and remove some of the landmines and obstacles they might encounter along the way. Just as a body builder finds it easier to lift 100 pounds after exercising for several month, so too will children with learning disabilities find it easier to face daily challenges when fortified with the muscles of determination and tenacity. Without these well-honed muscles, academics can seem to be insurmountable tasks. With them, goals feel attainable, and the learner's desire and interest to achieving success remain strong.

There are six habits that teachers and parents can exercise to help children develop the success skills necessary for their travels. They include labeling, describing, demonstrating, rehearsing, monitoring, and reinforcing the success skills.

Labeling the success skill. Parents and teachers must identify specific skills as success skills. All the success skills listed above should become integral parts of children's working vocabularies. Once when I suggested this to some early childhood teachers, one of them countered that a word like "perseverance" would be too hard for her children to learn or understand. However, another teacher who was aligned with this habit and introduced success skills to her class, proved her wrong in just a few short weeks. "I noticed one of my more oppositional students, a boy who rarely cleaned up during transition time, doing so the other day. When I encouraged his actions, he replied that he was persevering." Children can learn challenging words when teachers and parents accept the challenge to teach them. Make sure the words are discussed, illustrated, and continually addressed—in much the same way that reading, writing, and arithmetic are taught.

Describing the success skill. A label means nothing without a description. Children are not born with an understanding of self-control, initiative, or determination. A definition for each success skill is critical, and it must be described in concrete terms, meaningful to the child's level of understanding. In the course of conversations, children must be encouraged to use the word or its descriptions. Just recently, I listened to a teacher help her students learn patience. Different descriptions can be associated with patience, and it was exciting to hear her children state, "Patience is waiting for what you want." The children were already learning how to delay gratification and take turns, which eventually would instill within them patience to wait for their strengths to emerge.

Demonstrating the success skill. There are many ways to teach children, but few are better than demonstrating the skills to be learned. Success skills need modeling. On top of that, parallel talk is needed to reflect very concretely what is being modeled. I remember a time when I held a door open for a lady and her two children. The lady thanked me graciously while the two children failed to say a word. While the mom modeled respect, she did not use parallel talk and call attention to her behavior. Children do not often catch what we throw their way. Just as we help them learn to catch a ball, we must also help them learn to catch our comments. This is done through more obvious attempts. In this mom's case, she might stop and ask, "What did I say when the gentleman held the door for me? Now, what can you say? I want you to go back and thank the man."

Rehearsing the success skill. Rehearsal is the most exciting part of building success skills in children because they learn by doing. If your goal is to teach diligence, create teaching moments that encourage and draw attention to students being diligent. If you want children to grow muscles of determination, encourage and expect them to show determination throughout the day. Once children learn and understand one of the success skills, it must be applied in everyday life in order to become firmly rooted in children's actions. If you want children to read, expose them to reading. If you want children to show self-control, design scenarios that give them an opportunity to show self-control, and expect them to demonstrate such behavior.

Monitoring the success skill. Monitoring success skills is the most overlooked and underestimated part of the exercise program. One of the best ways to change the way children behave is to change the way they think. The mental messages presented earlier reflect this. Without diligent monitoring, success skills are often neglected on the back burner. Too often, concepts are introduced without follow-up, which is a very ineffective and inefficient way to teach, especially for struggling learners. Teachers and parents are encouraged to watch children's actions very carefully and to seize every opportunity to acknowledge their use of success skills.

Reinforcing the success skill. Children find it very satisfying to successfully accomplish tasks. I often find that children with learning problems love to apply determination, or one of the other success skills, if it is identified as a goal. Children who are normally discouraged over math problems may become more receptive to the challenge if they see their primary goal as showing determination and their secondary goal as solving the math problems. It is a way of reframing the expectation. The reinforcement can be a visual sign such as thumbs up or a verbal sign such as, "I see the determination in your work."

Success skills are vital components of helping children learn to succeed in life. Teaching these skills must not be done haphazardly or left to chance. When parents and teachers create a climate where children see success skills as their saving grace, the reading, writing, and arithmetic will more effectively fall into place.

CHAPTER SIX

EMBRACING THE GIFT

*I love you just the way you are. In fact, I love you
so much I am not willing to leave you that way.*

It was that time of year again—Lent. "What should I sacrifice?" I lamented. Each year I pledged to sacrifice something of great importance—usually one of my favorite foods. Historically, I failed about as often as I struggled on spelling tests. In fact, I probably expended more energy searching for sacrifices than making sacrifices. Nevertheless, this particular year I was bound and determined to find just the right sacrifice.

I was going through a very difficult period in my life. While I had faith in God for so many things, I had lost confidence in His willingness to help my son, Jim. I could recall the many times God propped me up and guided me through troubled waters: surviving quantitative analysis, the statistics comprehensive exam during my doctoral coursework, my dissertation, and so many other events I had struggled with. He seemed so close to me for a long time. That confidence had begun to crack. It started with simple yet unanswered prayers such as, "God, help Jim get chosen for major league baseball," "Bring Jim in contact with a wonderful person who can show him the same kind of friendship I experienced with Rodney and Chris," and "Help Jim on his schoolwork."

As time went by, my list of requests grew in number and my appeals grew in intensity. In my mind, the prayers were going unanswered. As God appeared to grow silent, my frustration grew tremendously until Jim's senior year in high school when a bully pushed him down on the basketball court and broke both arms. Why Jim? Through all of these tribulations, Jim never complained. I was the one agonizing and doubting. With each prayer that went unanswered (in my mind), I found myself with a greater and greater desire to make my requests known. These unanswered requests to God were like another form of failure on my part. "I can't even get God to look out for the best interests of my son." I imagined to myself, "God has either lost interest in Jim or He refuses to answer my pleas." Of course, neither was true, yet at the time, these feelings were mounting in my heart.

So it was that I found myself desperately searching that year to find just the right sacrificial lamb. I guess it was my attempt to get right with God. I thought that He would listen to my pleas and appeals on Jim's behalf. I thought, "My sacrifice shouldn't be something so traditional as giving up desserts, coffee or another of my favorite foods. They don't seem to measure up to my needs." I wondered, "What do I value that I would be willing to give up?"

I should not have welcomed my wife's participation in this struggle. God's sole purpose for Linda was to hold me accountable, or so it sometimes seemed. Linda quickly discerned, "Mark, you value time the most. It is the one thing you would hate to sacrifice." Linda was right. In fact, she was too right. I woke up every morning energized to seek new ways to achieve. Efficiency was my bosom buddy, and time was my dear friend. There was no time to waste and, fortunately, breakfast took very little time.

I failed to understand how time could serve as a sacrificial lamb. My second mistake was asking Linda to continue. She challenged, "Mark, what is Lent really about?" I sensed a lecture coming as I recoiled into a more defensiveness posture. Nevertheless, I began to think about her question. "I got it!" I exclaimed to myself. Time would become my sacrificial lamb. I still had to figure out what that meant and how it would happen.

Most of the time I spent with God was devoted to making my needs known. As mentioned, the majority of my needs revolved around Jim. Like me, Jim had grown up with a variety of learning challenges. Who better to take care of such challenges than Dad, the educator, counselor, empathizer, and identifier? I continually prayed for God's assistance and support to help me help Jim change certain behaviors that I didn't think were best for him. Those prayers very often reflected appeals and pleas for better things for Jim. I bombarded God with directives. Years of requests had already accumulated like barnacles on the sides of piers. The requests seemed to stick but go nowhere!

A few days later I visited Father Greg about my idea. I felt a bit pious, telling him about my decision to sacrifice time by spending thirty minutes each morning in prayer at the chapel. As I leaned forward on the sofa to get up and leave, Greg inquired, "Mark, what are your expectations?" Greg knew I was not a good candidate to sit still and listen to God for thirty minutes on a daily basis. He was right; I did have something in mind. I expressed confidently, "I plan to pray for Jim." Greg wasn't just going to accept that at face value. I began to squirm a bit, feeling cornered by his growing interest. "Tell me Mark, what kinds of requests do you have for God?" I told Father Greg about past prayers and how they seemed to go unanswered. I told him how I thought God might be more responsive under the present conditions, considering these prayers would be offered through sacrifice of my time at work. Greg's furrowed brow became even more pronounced. I glanced down at my watch, hoping Greg would sense the time pressure and let me off his hook, or even worse, God's hook.

Each of Father Greg's questions had a specific target, and the next was his most direct hit. "What will you do when God responds to your prayer and satisfies your idea of Jim's needs?" "I would start with the next request," I quickly retorted. "And then what?" Greg prodded. With a great sigh, the "ah hah" moment occurred. It felt like a sharp knife cutting through my heart. I doubled over with my hands cupped around my face. Wisely, Greg left me in silence, confident that I was not alone in my thoughts.

I began to experience a sense of conviction. I was not sacrificing time, and the chapel was not a conduit for sacrifice. Rather, I had made it into a bully pulpit, designed to capture God's attention under the guise of my devotion to Lent. I weakened as Greg gently nudged, "Mark, the sacrifice of time is a wonderful idea. But let that sacrifice be less about Jim and more about you. Walk hand-in-hand with your son, just as God walked hand-in-hand with His son. God embraced His son as a wonderful gift. See your son as that same gift. Ask God to teach you daily what it means to embrace Jim as a gift."

The light trickle of tears down my cheeks became more constant. Greg's nudge felt more like a fifty-pound jackhammer pulsating against my chest. I wanted to run. Yet, I could not move. While this meeting was not supposed to be about me, I felt surrounded by a spotlight directed on me and only me. Greg's next comment was piercing. "Mark, talk to me." His whisper reached down into the depths of my heart, bringing deep-rooted thoughts to the surface. I whispered back Greg's message, "See your son as a gift. Embrace your son as a gift." I replayed the message until it moved from my mind to my heart and into my very soul.

"A gift." I repeated more loudly. Of course, Jim was a gift. He was my son. Yet, Greg and I knew that the way I had been treating Jim, PROJECT was a more fitting word. I sat there dazed at the revelations that were surfacing. "How can a dad treat a son like a project?" I inquired. It was a rhetorical question. Greg knew it was not one for him to answer. My shame and guilt emerged like floodwater bursting through a dam as memories filled my consciousness of times when I had treated my son as a project, not a person. My transgressions were crystal-clear. There was nothing beautiful about my impatience regarding Jim's social awareness, academic progress, level of motivation, attention to detail, and/or organizational skills.

All along I had been treating Jim like a problem to be solved; he was a planned undertaking. How much time had I devoted to trying to make my son into someone else? How many times did I show little regard of the fruits of his labor or the wonderful qualities that he possessed? The thoughts reeked with badgering, "Jim, that is not good enough," or "Jim, you can do better."

As I began to understand the difference between treating Jim like a gift versus a project, my tears reappeared. Hardly audible to Father Greg, I reflected "Jim has always been my project. I have continually asked God to make changes and improvements in him. I have continually asked God to make Jim different. What was wrong with me that clouded my vision, that I didn't see his wonderful qualities?" I had realized so much about myself within a few short moments. Little did I know God was not yet finished with me.

Father Greg shifted the discussion about Jim to a more focused discussion about me and asked, "What have you failed to see in yourself that you also failed to see in your son?" The answer became as clear as a newly polished window. I had never seen myself as a gift. No wonder I couldn't see my son that way either.

A bewildered look fell upon my face as I exclaimed to Greg, "I am a project!" I recounted stories about times when I was tutored, examined, studied, and discussed. I remembered the countless hours sacrificed by Mom at the expense of her relationships with my dad and my brother and sisters. I remembered the worried look on Dad's face as he discussed my future. I also remembered the arguments between Dad and me when I failed to understand a point, despite his lengthy lecture on the subject. And I acutely remembered one time when Mom said, "Shhhh," when I informed her that I failed a particular examination. Mom was afraid that Dad would hear me.

What a painful yet wonderful revelation! Within a few moments, my bewildered look changed. I had long ago learned to reframe my thinking and was well skilled in it. Some people tend to see the thorns on a rose bush. Others see the blooms. I began to chuckle and then laugh heartily. "It has taken me fifty years to receive one of the greatest lessons in my life. Thank God!" Over the next few weeks, I sacrificed time kneeling before God asking that I learn to embrace myself as a gift. In so doing, I knew I could see Jim too as a gift, just the way he was.

During that Lent, I became born again to the unconditional love that we feel for our children at birth, when our only thoughts are for their safety rather than their performance. I began demonstrating a more accepting and less judgmental attitude towards others, especially Jim. I also became more accepting of myself. The grade book used to evaluate my achievements became less and less necessary, or important. I could accept my imperfections and mistakes more gracefully, and began to worry less about misguided perceptions. Most important, I began to see Jim in very much the same way. His strengths and wonderful qualities became more apparent as the blinders that had distorted his positive characteristics were removed. I began to see God's creation in Jim and realize that Jim was not a compilation of unfinished business. He was every bit the gift that he had been when born. Our relationship was transformed from that day forward.

~ ~ ~

I started this book ten years ago. Within days, I had quickly written 125 pages. My dear friend and great mentor, Dr. Dale Jordan, read the unpolished yet enthusiastically developed text. He urged, "Mark, place this text on the back burner. Let it sit as one would leave a bottle of wine to age. Grow in wisdom and knowledge. You will know when to dust off the pages and revisit your thoughts, feelings, and experiences."

For ten years, the dust settled on those 125 pages as I grew in knowledge and wisdom. It wasn't until two years ago that I learned one of my most important lessons. God taught me during that very special Lent to see my son and myself as gifts first rather than simply projects. It was then that I reveled in the good news that I could appreciate our giftedness while also shaping our growth. While I learned to love Jim and myself just the way each of us was, I came to understand that love also meant not being willing to leave him or me that way. Dr. Jordan was right. There was unfinished business.

That business was finished when I learned more about the challenges faced by teachers and parents, who sometimes try so hard that they overlook the giftedness in our struggling learners. While their intentions are good, I believe many children with learning problems are raised as projects and, subsequently, come to see themselves as projects.

My experiences have shaped my life, my actions, and my dreams. "I, too, have a dream." I have a dream that all children with learning challenges learn to embrace themselves, do their very best, make perseverance their bosom buddy, and make time their best friend. In my dream, children with learning challenges learn to move mountains with motivation, embrace their abilities and inabilities, taste defeat without quitting, replace thoughts of "I can't" with "I can", utilize their resources, and take more risks. In my dream, these children's lives are filled with meaning and purpose.

I also have a dream for parents, teachers, and other adults who come in contact with struggling learners. I have a dream that all adults see children with learning challenges as gifts first, that they see more of who the children are and less of who the children are not, and that they communicate an unconditional love regardless of children's performance. In my dream adults know that our children's very best does not require perfection, and recognize that any attempt to facilitate growth among the children should occur with complete affirmation and acceptance. When this happens, adults help children move mountains with motivation while also being satisfied with their present place on the mountain. They encourage children to embrace their abilities and inabilities by bathing them in the thought that through weakness we gain strength. Further, I dream that they replace their thoughts of "you can't" with "you can" and treat children as if they already were what they could be. Just as I long in my dream for children's lives to be filled with meaning and purpose, so do I dream this for the adults.

We are but a thought away from this dream. The Dr. Mark's Mental Messages were designed to encourage mighty thoughts that will walk us through an often treacherous jungle and into an oasis for children with learning challenges. Numerous pitfalls and snares can slow this success journey. The Dr. Mark's Injustices were designed to eliminate naiveté and anticipate the systemic evil that interferes with forward progress. A see-no-evil, hear- no-evil, and speak-no-evil allegiance is unacceptable. The injustices force out from the shadows of darkness into the light the thoughts and actions that misdirect the positive messages and obstruct the proactive strategies. The latter, the Dr. Mark's Strategies, were designed to release a sense of optimism and expectation that reflects no goal as too lofty or too ambitious. While adults of children with learning challenges cannot do everything, the strategies reflect those things we can do and do well.

In years past, I was in hiding. I had a secret. The voice that never went away repeated, "Mark, this is who you are not." Today, the hiding is over; the secret is gone. The old message has changed from one of hurt, despair, and resignation to a brighter and more confident message that says, "Mark, this is who you are and for that be well pleased." I now enjoy the view from the mountaintop regardless of my performance and accomplishments. While my appetite to achieve has not dissipated, my rationale has changed. I no longer perform for the next accolade or for recognition of my intellectual prowess. I strive to perform to bring about change in the lives of children and adults with learning challenges with whom I share so much. And I strive to affect the head, heart, and hands of those responsible for raising and/or teaching these children.

The truth has set me free and that freedom has become the wind beneath my wings. However, I will never be satisfied with my flight until those who teach and/or raise children with learning challenges become the wind beneath the wings of their children. At that time, I will truly enjoy the flight as many of us soar together with thoughts and feelings of affirmation, acceptance, affection, appreciation, and aspiration.

As I bring this book to a close, I am reminded of the conference where my wife and I were first told about our son's learning challenges. It was cold, calculated, and lacked any emotional concern for either Jim or us. I sat there stoically while my wife wept. Both of us felt betrayed by misguided thoughts and feelings. We had entered that room willing to exalt in our son's uniqueness but found ourselves defending our son's capacity, potential, and ability. My wife left the meeting adrift on a sea of unanswered questions and conflicting emotions. I left angered and alone. The next week when I met with the director of special education to explain my feelings, I found myself weeping and uncontrollably mourning not only my son's challenge, but also the challenges of all other struggling learners. I understood then the depth to which one can mourn for others.

Today, I am through mourning children born with learning challenges. I am through cooperating with the tunnel vision expressed by people who can only see the disabilities of our children. I am through turning a deaf ear to those who refuse to see children with challenges as cream ready to rise to the top. And I am through with the impossibility thinking that so easily and quickly caps the capabilities of our children.

Instead, I am here to exalt our children. This book demonstrates this exaltation. It is written for mothers, fathers, aunts and uncles, teachers and administrators who are ready to replace tears with tenacity, resignation with resolve, callousness with courage, and the determination to leave no stone unturned during this march toward justice and fairness for all.

Our nation has awakened to many new heroes. These heroes have been found in firefighters, police officers, flight attendants and pilots, soldiers, as well as everyday people who refused to be bystanders. I hope this book can awaken us to even more heroes - the people who show caring and compassion toward children regardless of their academic achievement or learning skills. How important is such heroism? Ask the struggling learner whose future has already been predicted with limitation. Ask the struggling learner whose reputation has been tarnished. Ask the struggling learner who is treated like a project. The people who are willing to resist such mistreatment and who champion struggling learners are our newly found heroes. Through their heroism, our children will not only live, but they will soar farther than they could ever imagine.

EPILOGUE

How does one end what took a lifetime to begin? I can think of no better way than to express my thoughts and feelings through this love letter to my mother. Mom died before I read this letter to her. I can only assume she will read it as she sits in heaven surrounded by the angels of giving—her kindred spirits. I believe I was destined to write a book for struggling learners and those responsible for their growth and development. More important, I believe Mom was destined to prepare me for that role. For that reason, I leave my final comments for Mom, who left only after she knew I was ready to soar.

Dear Mom,

During the past year, I have found a wonderful introduction to my speaking engagements. I tell a story about a man who entered the Pearly Gates only to find St. Peter. St. Peter graciously introduced himself and asked if the man had a question he wanted to ask. The man did have a question. He asked, "Who was the greatest general who ever lived?" St. Peter smiled with confidence, pointed to a man sitting on a cloud, and said, "There is the greatest general who ever lived." The man looked intently, drew back, and exclaimed, "Why, that could not be the greatest general who ever lived! I know that man. He was but a simple cobbler who worked at a small shop in my hometown." St. Peter responded, "Yes, you are right. The man was but a cobbler in a small shop, but had he been given the opportunity, he would have been the greatest general who ever lived."

Mom, this story reminds me of you. While I am not the greatest general who ever lived, I have accomplished small things in great ways. I have reinforced in the minds and hearts of children the fortitude to keep trying. I have reinforced in the minds and hearts of parents the idea to see their children as gifts rather than treating them as projects. I have reinforced in the minds and hearts of teachers the idea to see children's abilities rather than their disabilities. St. Peter remarked, "If he had been given the opportunity, he would have been a great general." This story is not really about people becoming great generals. This story is about those heroic people who become lifelines for those who struggle. This story is about you.

You see, Mom, you gave me the opportunities to make the happiness in my life possible. You are more than a mother to me. You are more than a dear friend. You are more than one who nurtured me as a mom naturally nurtures her children. You are my lifeline. You are the one who made tremendous sacrifices to teach me to not only dream, but to insist that those dreams could be fulfilled.

Mom, I am sorry I required so much attention during times when Dad, Kathy, Kristin, and Randy needed you as well. I never asked God that I be the struggling learner. I cannot even say that I am grateful that God provided me with such a blessing. However, I can say that I am grateful for you. I want to thank you, Mom, for your unconditional acceptance, your willingness to go beyond the call of duty, and your faith in my capabilities rather than everyday performances.

God willing, I am destined to affect the minds and hearts of struggling learners and those who support such learners through my speaking and writing. I realize more than ever that you were destined to prepare me. As I say in my conclusion to audiences, "I may be the one who stands before you, but I have a lifeline in my mom who speaks to you." Just as I pray to God before every speaking engagement that He speak to me and through me, I shall always know that you speak to me and through me as well. While your body may not be immortal, your gifts of sacrifice, encouragement, and persistence will sustain me throughout my lifetime and the lifetime of those affected by me because of you.

Mom, the song that I will play in my mind and heart during the next celebration of your life will be Bette Midler's "Wind Beneath My Wing." You are the wind beneath my wings. You have taught me to soar like the eagle. You have also shown me how to care about the heights to which others may soar.

Please know that I am O.K. with your transition from this life as we know it, to life as God knows it. Please know that I understand that very shortly you will soar in ways that our minds cannot comprehend and our hearts can only imagine. I cannot say that the floodgates of my heart will not speak loudly. I can say that my tears will celebrate your life and the wonderful union between our lives.

I love you Mom. I know that I must cooperate with the cutting of this second umbilical cord and let you go. God has reassured me that you have a wonderful place in His kingdom and that our union will not disappear. It will only change in a more God-like manner.

Since you will leave first, I want you to know a part of me will travel with you and a part of you will remain with me. It is a wonderful part for which my wife, children and children's children will be forever grateful. It is a wonderful part that could only be made in Heaven. Thank God for His creation. Thank God that He picked you before He picked me. His choice for me could not have been better.

With eternal love,
Your son, Mark

ABOUT THE AUTHOR

"You have seen me tossing and turning through the night. You have collected all my tears and preserved them in your bottle!"

Psalm 56:8 (The Living Bible)

In October, 1990 I conducted a workshop at the annual conference of the Arkansas Learning Disabilities Association. At the end of the first day, I followed a corridor toward the ballroom where an unfamiliar professor from Texas was scheduled to speak at a dinner meeting. As I rounded a corner, a young man came toward me, obviously looking for his destination. In explaining how to find the ballroom, I met Dr. Mark Cooper, the extraordinary man who has written this book about overcoming learning difficulties. Only half a dozen times during my 45 years helping struggling learners have I met a person equal to Dr. Mark in intelligence, integrity, and insight into what it is like to grow up with learning disabilities. This strikingly modest man has touched countless lives, young and old, with a depth of mercy and compassion that takes one's breath away. In his zeal to help struggling learners, Dr. Mark reminds me of an Old Testament prophet in his fearless defense of those who fall through the cracks of formal education.

As readers of *Bound and Determined* will discover, this man's candor and honest self-revelation are amazing and unexpected. Why would such a successful person reveal so much deeply personal and sensitive information about himself? Through a decade of friendship with this man, I have learned the secret of his compassion and the source of his strength. Readers of Dr. Mark's story will discover an incredible spiritual journey that began early in the author's life. Perhaps the best way to understand this man's secret is to ponder the spiritual truth expressed so poetically by the psalmist long ago. All of Dr. Mark's many tears have been collected in his Creator's bottle, where every moment of bitter pain has distilled into sweet wisdom. This wisdom is shared abundantly in the chapters of his book. It is rare indeed to find this quality of healing wisdom from one who has spent a lifetime overcoming his bent for learning difficulty.

Dale R. Jordan, Ph.D.
Learning Disabilities Consultant
Author of *Overcoming Dyslexia in Children, Adolescents, and Adults*

MARK J. COOPER, PH.D., L.P.C. is an associate professor in the department of early childhood and special education at the University of Central Arkansas and a licensed professional counselor. For more than thirty years, he has combated the toxicity that interferes with struggling learners and advocated a climate of success for those learners. His professional roles include teacher educator, school consultant, counselor, and public speaker.

Known better as Dr. Mark, he has been a contributing author to the *Autism Asperger's Digest,* a national magazine devoted to children and adults with autism spectrum disorders. He has also written on the topic of successful inclusion into the school environment of children from diverse backgrounds. This work has appeared in numerous other journals including *Focus on Autism and Other Developmental Disorders, Rural Special Education Quarterly,* and *Phi Delta Pi Record.* As a result of his commitment to children with learning disabilities, Mark has written editorials for local newspapers and for local and state newsletters. He uses such venues to encourage educators and administrators to demonstrate justice and fairness among students with learning disabilities. Mark frequently speaks at local, state, and national conferences on the topics related to helping children with learning problems become successful. He also speaks to assemblies of children and adolescents about thoughts important in their development of success skills.

Mark is married and has two children. Charlotte, the oldest, has a learning style and skills that fit perfectly within the school environment. His son, Jim, on the other hand, faces learning challenges and the residue associated with such challenges.

REFERENCES

Albert, L. (1996). *Cooperative discipline.* Circle Pines, Minnesota: American Guidance Service, Inc.

Anderson, P., & McKee, M. (1990). *Great quotes from great leaders.* Lombard, Illinois: Successories Publishing.

Badaracco, J. L., Jr. (2002). *Leading quietly: An unorthodox guide to doing the right thing.* Boston, Massachusetts: Harvard Business School Press.

Bartlett, J. (1962). *Familiar quotations: A collection of passages, phrases and proverbs traced to their sources in ancient and modern literature.* London: Macmillan & Co., Ltd.

Bennett, D., & Bennett, R. (1971). *The holy spirit and you: A study guide to the spirit filled life.* Plainfield, New Jersey: Logos International.

Boyer, E. L. (1995). *The basic school: A community for learning.* San Francisco, California: Jossey-Bass Inc., Publishers.

Brooks, R., & Goldstein, S. (2004). *The power of resilience: Achieving balance, confidence, and personal strength in your life.* Chicago: Contemporary Books.

Burns, D. D. (1993). You feel the way you think. *Ten days to self-esteem* (pp. 37–63). New York: William Morrow.

Cantor, N. (1990). From thought to behavior: "Having" and "doing" in the study of personality and cognition. *American Psychologist 45,* 735–750.

Cooper, M., & Mosley, M. (1999, March–April). Warning: Parental involvement may be hazardous. *Principal 78*(4), 73–74.

Covey, S. (1989). *The 7 habits of highly effective people.* New York: Simon & Schuster.

Devine, T, Seuk, J., & Wilson, A. (Eds). (2001). *Cultivating heart and character: Educating for life's most essential goals.* Chapel Hill, NC: Character Development Publishing.

Dickens, C. (1868). *The great expectations.* London: Chatman and Hall.

Fisher, B. & Thomas, B. (1996). *Real dream teams: Seven practices used by world- class team leaders to achieve extraordinary results.* Delray Beach, Florida: St. Lucie Press.

Fisher, G., & Cummings, R. (1995). *When your child has LD: A survival guide for parents.* Minneapolis, Minnesota: Free Spirit Publishing.

Fletcher-Janzen, E., & De Pry, R (2003). *Social competence and character: Developing IEP goals, objectives, and interventions.* Longmont, Colorado: Sopris West.

Glasser, W. (1997). Choice theory and student success. *Education Digest 63,* 16–36.

Goleman, D. (1995). *Emotional intelligence: Why it can matter more than IQ.* New York: Butnam Books.

Groopman, J. (2004). *The anatomy of hope: How people prevail in the face of illness.* New York: Random House.

Hock, M., Schumaker, J., & Deshler, D. (2003). *Possible selves: Nurturing student motivation.* Lawrence, Kansas: Edge Enterprises.

Katz, L. (1992). What should young children be learning? *ERIC Digest.* Urbana, Illinois: ERIC Clearinghouse on Elementary and Early Childhood Education.

Katz, L. (1993). *Dispositions as educational goals.* ERIC Digest. Urbana, Illinois: ERIC Clearinghouse on Elementary and Early Childhood Education.

Lavoie, R. (1989). *Understanding learning disabilities: How difficult can this be? The F.A.T. city workshop* [Motion Picture]. United States: PBS Video.

Levine, M. (2002). *A mind at a time*. New York: Simon & Schuster.

Levinson, H. N. (1988). *Smart but feeling dumb: The challenging new research on dyslexia and how it may help you*. New York: Warner Books, Inc.

Levinson, H. N. (1992). *Total concentration: How to understand attention deficit disorders*. New York: M. Evans & Co.

Markus, H., & Nurris, P. (1986). Possible selves. *American Psychologist, 41,* 954–969.

Maxwell, J. C. (1997). *The success journey: The process of living your dreams*. Nashville, Tennessee: Thomas Nelson Publishers, Inc.

Meyer, D. J., & Vadasy, P. F. (1994). *Sibshops: Workshops for siblings of children with special needs*. Baltimore, Maryland: Paul H. Brooks Publishing.

Pocok, A., Lambros, S., Karvonen, M., Test, D. T., Algozzine, B., Wood, W., et al. (2002, March) Successful strategies for promoting self-advocacy among students with LD: The lead group. *Intervention in School and Clinic, 209*–216.

Rich, D. (1992). *MegaSkills* (Rev. ed.). New York: Houghton Mills.

Rogoff, B., Gauvain, M., & Ellis, S. (1990). Development viewed in cultural context. In P. Light, S. Sheldon & M. Woodhead (Ed.), *Learning to think*. London: Routledge, 292–239.

Schweitzer, A. (1963). *Out of my life and thought*. New York: New American Library, 74.

Seligman, M. (1991). *The family with a handicapped child* (2nd ed.). Needham Heights, Massachusetts: Simon & Schuster.

Shure, M. B., Digeronimo, T. Foy & Aher, J. (2000). *Raising a thinking child workbook: Teaching young children how to resolve everyday conflicts and get along with others*. Champaign, Illinois: Research Press.

Silver, L. B. (1998). *The misunderstood child: Understanding and coping with your child's learning disabilities* (3rd ed.). New York: Three Rivers Press.

RESOURCES FOR PARENTS AND FAMILY MEMBERS
Parent Training and Information Centers

As a parent of a struggling learner, a teacher educator, counselor, school consultant, and active member of the Learning Disability Association, I frequently needed support and assistance regarding advocacy matters for children with learning disabilities. Janice Meyer, Director of Partners Resource Network, Inc., performed a tremendous service keeping parents and teachers informed about children's rights.

The Partner's Resource Network team was a member of a bigger team—the Parent Training and Information Centers (PTI). A primary responsibility for the centers is to provide training and information to parents of children and adolescents with disabilities. They also work closely with professionals who work with their families. This assistance and support help parents work more effectively with professional educators responsible for the education and welfare of children and adolescents with disabilities.

The PTI team in Beaumont, Texas was thorough in their understanding about children and adolescents with disabilities and offered tremendous support and encouragement. Each state is home to at least one parent center. A listing of Parent Resource Centers can be obtained by typing "parent training and information centers" into the web browser of any computer. I encourage readers to contact the nearest PTI for information about parent support and other local services.

Recommended Readings

Abourjilie, C. (2000). *Developing character for classroom success: Strategies to increase responsibility, achievement and motivation in secondary students.* Chapel Hill, North Carolina: Character Development Publishing.

Achieving true success: How to build character as a family. (2001). Oklahoma City, Oklahoma: International Association of Character Cities.

Boyer, W.A.R., & Rumson, B. (2000). *Developing optimism: Teaching children the value of positive thinking.* Torrance, California: Fearon Teacher Aids.

Brooks, R. (2000). Self-esteem and resilience: A precious gift for our children. *The child information and resource guide* (pp. 34–37). Landover, MD: CHADD.

Brooks, R. (2002). *Raising resilient children: A curriculum to foster strength, hope, and optimism in children.* Chicago: Contemporary Books.

Brooks, R. (2004). *The self-esteem teacher.* Loveland, Ohio: Treehaus Communications, Inc.

Brooks, R., & Goldstein, S. (2003). *Nurturing resilience in our children: Answers to the most important parenting questions.* Chicago: Contemporary Books.

Brooks, R. & Goldstein, S. (2004). *The Power of resilience: Achieving balance, confidence, and personal strength in your life.* Chicago: Contemporary Books.

Citro, T. A. (Ed.). (1998). *The experts speak: Parenting the child with learning disabilities.* Weston, MA: Learning Disabilities Worldwide.

Citro, T. A. (Ed.). (2004). *Many shades of success: Other views of post-secondary options.* Weston, MA: Learning Disabilities Worldwide.

Cooper, M., & Griffith, K. (2000, March-April). The heart and soul of inclusion: Preparing classmates to care. *Autism Asperger's Digest.*

Covey, S. (1989). *The 7 habits of highly effective people.* New York: Simon & Schuster.

Deshler, D., Schumaker, J., Lenz, B., Bulgre, J., Hock, M., Knight, J., et al. (2001). Ensuring content area learning by secondary students with learning disabilities. *Learning Disabilities Research & Practice, 16*(2), 96–108.

Fisher, G., & Cummings, R. (1995). *When your child has LD: A survival guide for parents.* Minneapolis, Minnesota: Free Spirit Publishing.

Fletcher-Janzen, E., & DePry, R. (2003). *Social competence and character: Developing IEP goals, objectives, and interventions.* Longmont, Colorado: Sopris West.

Gardner, H. (1999). *Intellect reframed: Multiple intelligences for the 21st century.* New York: Basic Books.

Glasser, W. (1998). *Choice theory: A new psychology of personal freedom.* New York: Harper Perennial.

Glasser, W. (2000). *Counseling on choice theory.* New York: Quill Publishing.

Glasser, W. & Glasser, C. (1999). *The language of choice theory.* New York: Harper Perennial.

Goleman, D. (1995). *Emotional intelligence.* New York: Bantam.

Greenberger, D., & Padesky, C. (1995). *Mind over mood.* New York: Guilford Press.

Groopman, J. (2004). *The anatomy of hope: How people prevail in the face of illness.* New York: Random House.

Hallowell, E., & Ratey, J. J. (1994). *Driven to distraction: Recognizing and coping with attention deficit disorder from childhood through adulthood.* Toronto, Canada: Random House.

Hock, M., Schumaker, J., & Deshler, D. (2003). *Possible selves: Nurturing student motivation.* Lawrence, Kansas: Edge Enterprises.

Jordan, D. (2002) *Overcoming dyslexia in children, adolescents, and adults.* Dallas, Texas: Pro-Ed.

Klein, S. D., & Schive, K (2001) *You will dream new dreams: Inspiring personal stories by parents of children with disabilities.* New York: Kensington Publishing Co.

Kouzes, J. M. & Posner, B. Z. (1999). *Encouraging the heart: A leader's guide to rewarding and recognizing others.* San Francisco: Jossey-Bass.

Lavoie, R. (1989). *Understanding learning disabilities: How difficult can this be? The F.A.T. city workshop* [Motion Picture]. United States: PBS Video.

Lavoie, R. (1994). *Learning disabilities and social skills: Last one picked, first one picked on* [Motion Picture]. United States: PBS Video.

Lavoie, R. (2001). Poker chips & self-esteem. *Texas Key,* 1044, 9–16.

LeGette, H. R. (1999). *Parents, kids & character: 21strategies to help your children develop good character.* Chapel Hill, North Carolina: Character Development Publishing.

Levine, M. (2002). *A mind at a time.* New York: Simon & Schuster.

Levinson, H. N. (1988). *Smart but feeling dumb: The challenging new research on dyslexia and how it may help you.* New York: Warner Books. Inc.

Mannix, D. (1993). *Social skills activities for special children.* West Nyack, New York: The Center for Applied Research in Education.

Maxwell, J. C. (1997). *The success journey: The process of living your dreams.* Nashville, Tennessee: Thomas Nelson Publishers, Inc.

Meyer, D. J,. & Vadasy, P. F. (1994). *Sibshops: Workshops for siblings of children with special needs.* Baltimore, Maryland: Paul H. Brooks Publishing.

Seligman, M. (2002). *Authentic happiness.* New York: Free Press.

Seligman, M. E. P. (1990). *Learned optimism: How to change your mind and your life.* New York: Pocket Books.

Shure, M. B., Digeronimo, T. Foy & Aher, J. (2000). *Raising a thinking child workbook: Teaching young children how to resolve everyday conflicts and get along with others.* Champaign, Illinois: Research Press.

Sicoone, F., & Lopez, L. (2000). *Educating the heart: Lessons to build respect and responsibility.* Needham Heights, Massachusetts: A Pearson Education Company.

Silver, L. B. (1998). *The misunderstood child: Understanding and coping with your child's learning disabilities* (3rd ed.). New York: Three Rivers Press.

Silver, L.B. (Host), & Citro, T. A. (Producer/Director). (1999). *Profiles of success: Successful adults achieving with learning disabilities* [Motion Picture]. United States: Learning Disabilities Worldwide.

Silver, L. B, & Brooks, R. (Hosts), & Citro, T. A. (Producer/Director). (2000). *Portraits of success: Fostering hope and resilience in individuals with learning disabilities* [Motion Picture}. United States: Learning Disabilities Worldwide.

Young, M. E. (2001). *Learning the art of helping: Building blocks and techniques* (2nd ed.). Upper Saddle River, New Jersey: Prentice Hall.